This Book Belongs To
Sarah Bellows

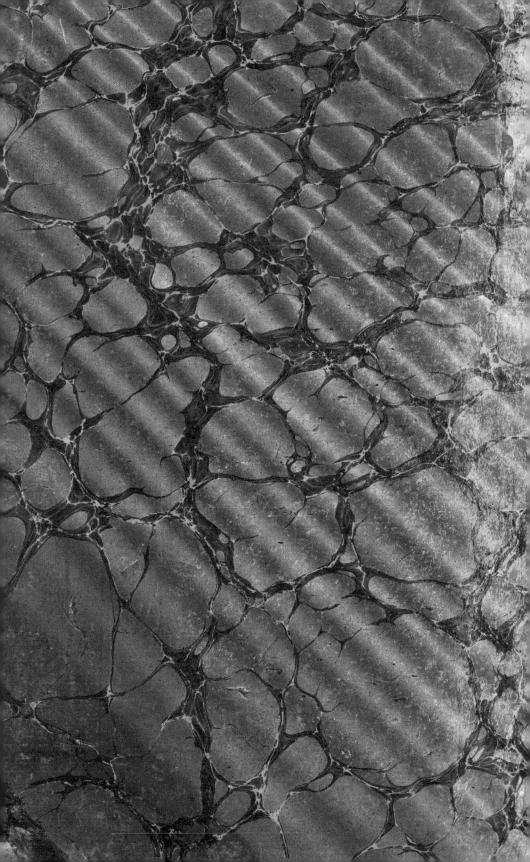

SCARY STORIES

TO TELL IN THE DARK

•THE HAUNTED NOTEBOOK•
OF SARAH BELLOWS

Respectfully, Dr Ephraim Bellows

Checks to be made payable to Pennhurst Hospital, and all remit-
letters relating to clothing must be sent to our care.

Sarah Bell

189.

STATE OF PENNSYLVANIA } 89.
COUNTY OF MILL VALLEY

The petitioner above named, being fi

true .... / .... verily believe.

{D.–1}

SCARY STORIES

TO TELL IN THE DARK

• THE HAUNTED NOTEBOOK • OF SARAH BELLOWS

WRITTEN BY RICHARD ASHLEY HAMILTON

BASED ON THE SCREENPLAY BY
DAN HAGEMAN & KEVIN HAGEMAN

SCREEN STORY BY
GUILLERMO DEL TORO AND
PATRICK MELTON & MARCUS DUNSTAN

INSIGHT ◉ EDITIONS
SAN RAFAEL · LOS ANGELES · LONDON

INSIGHT
EDITIONS

PO Box 3088
San Rafael, CA 94912
www.insighteditions.com

Find us on Facebook: www.facebook.com/InsightEditions
Follow us on Twitter: @insighteditions

Library of Congress Cataloging-in-Publication Data available.

ISBN: 978-1-68383-853-1

Publisher: Raoul Goff
President: Kate Jerome
Associate Publisher: Vanessa Lopez
Creative Director: Chrissy Kwasnik
Senior Editor: Greg Solano
Managing Editor: Lauren LePera
Senior Production Manager: Greg Steffen

Designed by *the*BookDesigners

ROOTS of PEACE

🌲 REPLANTED PAPER

Insight Editions, in association with Roots of Peace, will plant
two trees for each tree used in the manufacturing of this book.
Roots of Peace is an internationally renowned humanitarian
organization dedicated to eradicating land mines worldwide and
converting war-torn lands into productive farms and wildlife
habitats. Roots of Peace will plant two million fruit and nut
trees in Afghanistan and provide farmers there with the skills
and support necessary for sustainable land use.

Manufactured in Canada by Insight Editions

10 9 8 7 6 5 4 3 2 1

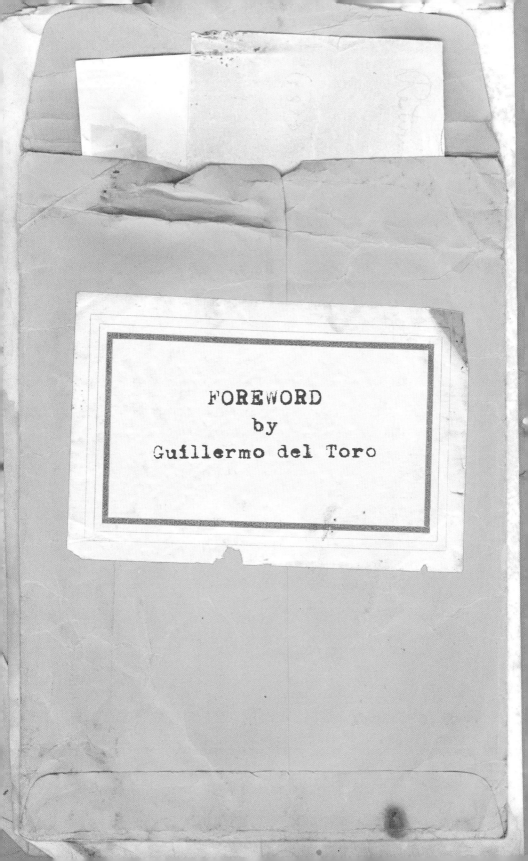

FOREWORD
by
Guillermo del Toro

FOREWORD
by
Guillermo del Toro

Scary stories—they work because they are universal.
They are told in every country and every language and
always with the deceitful simplicity of a campfire tale.

I discovered *Scary Stories to Tell in the Dark* more
than thirty years ago. I saw a copy of the first volume
in a used bookstore in San Antonio, Texas. I read it,
from cover to cover, sitting in the aisle. Then, I came
back and read it again—and gawked, transfixed at the
impossibly tenuous illustrations of Stephen Gammell.

His graphite-and-pencil illustrations feel as if
they're rendered in tendrils of smoke and shadow. True
snapshots of an alternate reality, where things go
bump in the night.

When I was approached to make the film based on
the books, I knew two things: One, this would not be an
anthology. It needed to be thematically of a piece and
deliver characters we cared for. Two, I wanted to trans-
late the creatures dreamt by Gammell unto the screen.

To do so, we required the best sculptors I know in
the makeup effects business to create the characters as
Gammell depicted them. Spectral Motion, Mike Elizalde's
company and one of the foremost FX houses in the world,
spearheaded the task by selecting with me the two best
creators we know: Mike Hill and Norman Cabrera. Over
several months, we worked hard to make sure that the
three-dimensional suits and prosthetics we delivered
were faithful to the images they were rendering.

We partnered with MR. X in Canada to blend VFX
seamlessly with physical suits and makeup FX. The
result is before you.

10

Having used the *Book of Crossroads* in *Pan's Labyrinth*—a book that reveals the reader's fate only seconds before it happens—I decided to pursue the idea of a different kind of book: a book of stories that reads *you*—that figures out what makes each reader tick and then renders the ultimate scary story for each one. The author of the book, herself a misunderstood girl—Sarah Bellows—is maligned by tales people have told about her ... Thus the theme of the film revealed itself: the importance of stories and how they shape who we are.

I decided then to set the film in the 1960s, a time of crucial importance for North America and a time when kids were dying in a war far, far away ... a war they were told was important but which they seldom understood.

We are told by the media that childhood should be a perfect experience. But if you grow up in a perfect environment, you are being prepared for a world that is not real. The great thing about Schwartz and Gammell's *Scary Stories* is that it acknowledges the scary aspects of the world.

The man behind the camera, André Øvredal is, in my estimation, one of the great stylists in the horror genre. His images and camera staging are refined but not artificial. After one production meeting, André laid out his credo for *Scary Stories* to me: "I want the everyday to be real," he explained, "so the extraordinary stands out." That is opposite of what I would have done. But I knew the moment he said it he was right. Our journey to accomplish that goal was a complex but rewarding one.

I hope you enjoy reading the book you now have in your hands and I pray with all my might that it does not read you in return ...

—Guillermo del Toro
June 2019, Toronto, Ontario

11

Harold.

When it
drove thei
mounta
the co
down t
Th
day t
Tomm
At night
lived. The
and went
Then T
"Let's m
would b
"It s
a farmer
sacks stuf
like Harol
dark h
gave it
Each
Harold to
Each night t
get ruined if
When they w
to him. One of the
vegetables growing to
making believe he w
voice, "Very slowly."
Harold.

That Halloween, young Thomas Milner considered running over the scarecrow.

The thought had occurred to him many times before. Ever since he'd gotten his learner's permit, Tommy had fantasized about using his car like one of the threshers on the family farm. His cruel mouth would split into a smile and his knuckles would whiten on the steering wheel as he imagined mowing down the straw man like some oversized bale of wheat.

Yes, Tommy had always hated that scarecrow. Hated the tattered, sun-bleached clothes it wore. Hated the way its cut-out eyes always remained in shadow, always seemed to be staring at Tommy like two unblinking sockets. Hated the way it never actually scared away any crows (although, truth be told, Tommy did like how the big black birds made the useless dummy their own personal toilet). But most of all, Tommy hated the scarecrow's name.

Harold.

Tommy's mom had named the ugly thing not long after she assembled it from old clothes, burlap, and hay. And Tommy knew how much his mom liked to play with dolls, even as a grown woman. Just as Tommy knew that's what she'd call the scarecrow. He could've seen that name coming from an acre away.

The sound of the Pontiac's tires scratching against gravel brought Tommy back to the present. He jerked his steering wheel to the side, returning the car to the road and off its collision course with Harold.

"Next time, ugly," Tommy muttered, smelling the liquor on his own breath.

As he turned down the driveway and drove past Harold, the scarecrow's moonlit face just stared, same as always, from its crooked stake in the ground. Reaching the farmhouse at the end of the drive, Tommy killed the engine and staggered out of the driver's seat. He reeked of beer, ashes, and something far more pungent.

"Punks are dead," Tommy slurred at the brown streaks on his jeans and letterman jacket.

His scorched fingers still smarted from where they'd swatted against the flaming paper bag. Tommy had picked up a couple of guys from their varsity team and that girl he was seeing on the side, Ruth. Although the Pontiac Catalina was never a car Tommy would've chosen for himself, he had to admit it held a lot of teenagers. The plan was to have a little fun with a few of the trick-or-treaters wandering around Mill Valley. Then they'd all head to the Gorge drive-in so Tommy could drink more and he and Ruth could have a little fun of a different kind. And then Tommy would take Ruth to dinner, like he promised. If he felt like it. Maybe. Or maybe Tommy would see if the Wolverton girl was up for a little fun instead.

But then those three losers from school had to ruin everything. They ambushed Tommy and his friends, egging his car and tossing a burning paper bag through the open window. It landed on Tommy's lap, and he slapped out the flames quick enough. For a moment, Tommy figured his quick reflexes might impress Ruth and make her even more infatuated with him. That's when the stench hit Tommy, and he realized the paper bag hadn't been empty. Brown stuff coated his hands and clothes. Growing up on a farm, Tommy had smelled all kinds of scat. Pigs'. Horses'. Cows'. Chickens'. But this wasn't any animal's. This came from a person.

The memory made Tommy gag in his driveway.

Somehow, he managed to keep it down. He looked at
the fresh dent in his fender and the scratches on
the hood's paint job, all from when Tommy crashed
into a fence.

"It was the smoke in my eyes," Tommy had told
Ruth and the others after the fender bender. "From
the bag."

And that's what Tommy continued to tell himself outside the farmhouse. He hadn't had too much
to drink. He hadn't lost control of the car. Tommy
Milner was always in control.

Tommy thought he heard a laugh. He glared across
the cornfield at Harold. The way the moon cast shadows across the scarecrow's face made him look like
he was smiling.

It.

Like it was smiling, Tommy corrected himself.

Another autumn wind blew through the stalks, and
Tommy heard more laughter. He turned his back on
Harold and stumbled toward the porch, only to be
greeted at the front door by his mother. She drew
her bathrobe tighter around the nape of her neck,
shuddering at the rising chill.

So much for hitting the hay, thought Tommy.

"It's late," barked Mrs. Milner.

"It's Halloween," Tommy said back.

All the way across the porch, Mrs. Milner could
smell her son's boozy breath. She even recognized
the brand of beer.

Like father, like son, thought Mrs. Milner.

"You were supposed to deliver eggs to the
Wolvertons," she said instead.

Just hearing the word *eggs* made Tommy think
of his defiled Pontiac. The yolks that splattered
against his windshield had clearly been rancid. A
whiff of sulfur, coupled with the feces still stain-
ing his prized jacket, induced another wave of nausea in Tommy's guts. He forced himself not to vomit

and not to talk back to his mother. Tommy didn't
need another lecture from some disapproving
old lady. He was a man now, just turned eighteen.
Independent. Enlisted. Come graduation from Mill
Valley High, Tommy would be leaving their farm,
leaving their boring dead-end town, and leaving
their family. Well, what was left of their family.
After a few weeks of basic, he and his platoon
would be well on their way to distant fields of
another kind, mowing down a different sort of tar-
get altogether.

The happy thought settled Tommy's stomach. He
turned on his heels, ignoring Mrs. Milner's glare,
and flippantly sauntered off toward the barn.
Along the way, Tommy kicked aside one of the
pea-brained chickens that riddled the farm, then
sensed another pair of eyes boring into him. This
felt different from his mother's usual glower.
Looking over his shoulder, Tommy saw Mrs. Milner
had left the porch and gone back inside the farmhouse. The only figure left staring at him now was
Harold, that same mirthless grin on his false face.

Its.

Its false face, Tommy reminded himself.

His ruined jacket scuffed against the barn door
as he shoved it open. The place reeked of stale hay,
mildew, and urine. He heard skittering sounds in
the dark, like bird talons on corrugated metal. Or
pitchfork tines against something just as hard, like
rock. Or bone. Tommy didn't know why that image
popped into his head. He wasn't a poet or writer like
that girl. ... What's her name? The one who ignored
Tommy's repeated invitations to join him under the
bleachers. The one who helped those other two nerds
lob the flaming bag into his Catalina.

After the crash, Tommy and his pals had chased
the three of them—the stuck-up girl, that beanpole

with the divorced parents, and Ruth's bratty little
brother—to the drive-in. Yes, Tommy made it to the
Gorge after all, although his definition of fun had
changed considerably by that point. He spotted the
three losers inside a parked '63 Rambler Ambassador
with some wetback greaser. The four of them refused to
get out of the car no matter how hard Tommy slammed
on the windows. After a while, Tommy gave up. Mostly to
shut up the drive-in manager, but also to dupe those
little vandals into feeling safe. This was a classic
combat tactic, as Tommy had been reading in the mate-
rials supplied by the recruiting office. This was how a
soldier coaxed an enemy out of hiding. This was war.

And so Tommy waited, forcing Ruth to stay with
him even after his lettermen pals departed, until the
Rambler drove away from the drive-in. The Pontiac
followed the wetback's car, headlights off, until they
reached the old Bellows place at the edge of town.
Tommy waited for the four kids to go inside the
dilapidated heap of a house before running over to
the empty Rambler.

He smashed its windshield, slashed its tires, and
wrenched as many cables out of the engine block as
his furious hands could hold. He then broke open the
trunk, hoping for something of value to steal—but
found a can of spray paint instead. Over Ruth's pro-
tests, he wrote the word *wet* on the Rambler's hood and
the word *back* on its burgled trunk.

Tommy snickered in the barn, just as he had after
finishing his graffiti earlier that night. Maybe he was
a poet or a writer after all. Just like what's-her-name.
With a final chuckle, Tommy fumbled for the barn's
overhead light and turned it on. The bulb immediately
burned out with a loud *pop* that made him flinch.

Darkness returned to the barn. Yet this darkness felt different from the one that had preceded
the flickering bulb. It felt deeper, heavier, as if a
shadow descended upon the entire structure. Tommy's

alcohol-addled mind now pictured a colossal crow
landing on the barn roof, its black wings blotting
out the moon like some unforeseen eclipse.

Tommy muttered angrily and crossed over to the
chicken coop. Still consumed by his own seething
resentment, he nearly missed the shape that appeared
in the water trough beside him. A persistent drip from
the leaky faucet used to wash out milking pails had
disturbed the water's surface. But the water suddenly
went as still and smooth as glass. In the reflection,
Tommy thought he saw a pale shape.

Once again Tommy flinched. But when he looked back
at the trough, it was a murky, rippling pool once
more. He noticed he was sweating in the cold, smelling
the liquor through his pores. He opened the hutch and
gathered a dozen eggs, his movements faster than they
had been a moment ago.

Fine, thought Tommy, his mind racing as fast as his
hands. *I'll deliver eggs to the Wolvertons. Then I'll see
if their daughter's still up for more fun than Ruth
and what's-her-name.*

He shuttered the coop, deposited the eggs in their
basket, and got up to leave. But the sight of blood
made Tommy stop. A chicken carcass festered on the
ground, gore pasting straw and loose feathers to what
remained of its body. Tommy looked to the side and
saw the perpetrators: The other chickens had pecked it
to death. Bits of down and flesh clung to their red-
dened beaks. Their beady eyes glinted in the night,
staring at him as if he were less than a man. Tommy
heard another skittering sound, followed by the keen
of a faraway voice.

The Milner boy spun around with a start. Another
autumn wind blew through the barn, rattling its ramshackle walls and riling the crows in the rafters. The
murder flapped and cawed. Tommy took the eggs and left
for the last time. He went back toward the Pontiac and
reached for the driver's-side door handle. But when he

looked up at the porch, he saw the silhouette of a woman.

"Jesus!" cried Tommy, nearly dropping half a dozen.

He caught the eggs before their shells dashed on the driveway, then faced the front of the farmhouse again. The woman stepped closer. It was his mother, her robe wrapped about her like a shroud, her stern posture

backlit by the bug zapper hanging on the porch.

"What do you think you're doing?" demanded Mrs. Milner.

"Delivering the eggs," Tommy said pointedly.

"Not in my car," Mrs. Milner said before she looked closer at the damaged Pontiac. "My car. And your clothes. Is that chocolate? What'd you do?"

"Ma, it wasn't me," Tommy shouted back.

"May as well have been!" shrieked his mother. "When I lend you my property, you have a responsibility to return it the way you found it."

"But—" Tommy began.

"You'd better clean that mess before your father sees," said Mrs. Milner.

Tommy gestured—*fine!*—with an impatient wave of his hands and made toward the hose and bucket at the side of their home. But he stopped in midstep when his mother cleared her throat and added, "After you've delivered those eggs to the Wolvertons."

"How am I supposed to do that without my ca—"

"*My car*," Mrs. Milner insisted. "And you can do it the way you did before you learned to drive. And drink."

She pointed across the cornfield to another farmhouse about a mile away. Its lit windows twinkled remotely from the top of the hill.

"Walk," said Tommy's mother.

Sighing, he clutched the egg basket tighter and stomped away from the porch. Tommy took the path that cut through the cornfield, his pickled feet stumbling over the furrows plowed into the earth. He walked past Harold, still on the pike, still staring.

For a second time that night, Tommy considered inflicting harm on the scarecrow. It wouldn't have been the first time he used him—*it*—as a punching bag. Tommy often snuck off to the field and worked out his aggressions on the lumpy straw figure, just as Tommy's father had demonstrated, in his own way, so often before. And on this night, Harold was in the way, and Tommy was in a mean mood.

"Eat shit, Harold," said Tommy before continuing on his way.

Typical, he thought as he marched through the field. *Give me your car, only to take it away. Lay out clothes for me every morning like I'm still some little kid. I know what you're doing. Trying to control me. Keep me from leaving for the war. Keep me clinging to your apron strings. Keep me like another one of your little dress-up dol—*

Tommy's chain of thought broke off abruptly. His eyes widened. He saw that he was walking past Harold again. Still on the pike. Still staring.

Confused, Tommy turned around. He had just left Harold fifty feet back ... hadn't he? Maybe Tommy hadn't traveled as far as he thought. Maybe he'd had more beers than he thought.

Spotting the Wolvertons' lit farmhouse in the distance, he trudged ahead. Maize swayed all around him. Another gust blew through the field, fluttering the leaves and buffeting the caterpillars feasting upon them. Tommy tried to keep his eyes on the path ahead, tried to put one foot in front of the other. The sooner he delivered these damn eggs, the sooner he could clean the Pontiac—*his* Pontiac—and put this whole stupid night behind him. But Tommy found his gaze drawn to the periphery. He saw a lone, long hair entwined with the silk on a nearby ear of corn. It shimmered silver in the moonlight.

Unsettled, Tommy backed away from the kinked, glowing thread and into a new clearing amid the crops. His legs faltered. His eyes grew wider still. For Tommy Milner encountered the scarecrow pike once again. Only, this time, the large wooden stake stood empty, with Harold nowhere in sight.

What the hell? thought Tommy as he blinked at the vacant pike in a stupor.

He heard a rustle in the nearby corn rows. Tommy jumped, losing sight of the Wolverton house on the hill and his general sense of direction. It felt as if he'd wandered into one of the mazes they have at the fall harvest festivals. But fear sobered him quickly, and Tommy knew this was no carnival. Forcing himself to calm and take control, Tommy rediscovered the pathway that brought him there. He took a step. Stopped. Squinted.

A body stood down the path. High above, the moon emerged from a cloud, and its renewed luster illuminated the cornfield. Tommy saw that the body on the path was no woman, no trick of the light, no figment of his inebriated imagination.

It was Harold.

The scarecrow stood on his—ITS—own. No pike. Still staring.

Tommy felt warmth trickle between his legs and scrambled backward. His limbs, numb and unresponsive, tripped over each other, and Tommy fell. The eggs he'd been carrying smashed on the loamy ground. Getting back onto his feet, Tommy whipped his head around and looked back at the path.

Harold stood ten feet closer, his sutured face leering in the moonlight.

Tommy's heart seized when the scarecrow took one jerky step forward. It reminded him of how a toddler learns to walk.

Harold took another step, this one surer than the last.

"Oh, shit!" Tommy blurted.

He backpedaled farther. Yet Harold lurched closer still, each footfall gaining in confidence.

Tommy wished he'd been deployed to boot camp

yesterday. He broke into a run, stomping over the broken eggs and following the path back to his parents' farm. After a few sprints, Tommy looked back over his shoulder, his vision blurred, delirious.

Harold's menacing frame followed, finding its footing as it shambled ever closer to Tommy.

As he turned a sharp corner, Tommy's soles skidded on the soil and flew out from under him. He tumbled hard against the ground and came to a stop mere inches from the business end of a pitchfork. The tines sparkled before his eyes, almost hypnotic in the night.

Tommy shook his head and pushed himself off the dirt yet again. He studied the pitchfork, the way it'd been placed across the path almost like one of those tripwires the guerrillas used overseas. Almost like ... a prank.

And just like that, Tommy knew what was happening. Confidence coursed through his veins as he claimed the pitchfork off the field. Those four peckerwoods somehow busted out of the Bellows place, and this nonsense with the scarecrow was more of their dress-up, trick-or-treat horseshit. This was their pathetic version of revenge.

Tommy pivoted with the pitchfork and discovered Harold right behind him on the path, right where he expected him to be. The scarecrow towered over Tommy. This had to be that tall kid—the beanpole from earlier. Ruth's turd of a brother probably helped him into the getup. Probably stuffed in extra straw so his friend looked like he had some muscle on him for once.

"Whoever's in there, I'm gonna kick your ass!" Tommy shouted.

Harold stared.

Tommy plunged the pitchfork into the scarecrow, right into his chest.

Harold. Stared.

Removing the pitchfork with ease, Tommy goggled

at its forked end. There was no blood there. Just
bits of straw. If this wasn't one of what's-her-name's
freak-show friends, then—

Tommy dropped the pitchfork and bolted for his
house. He felt an immediate and overriding urge to
cry out for his mommy. And then he felt a strange
pressure run through his chest, followed by an odd
weightless feeling in his legs.

Looking down, Tommy Milner saw the pitchfork
protruding through his own ribs. Tommy's jaws
clicked in shock, and he looked back at the straw
man who had stabbed him.

Harold.

Just.

Stared.

It never occurred to Tommy how odd it was that
he didn't feel pain in the moment. He merely pushed
himself off the pitchfork and collapsed onto the
hardscrabble path. He touched his perforated chest,
expecting to feel his fingers slicked with crimson.

But no blood issued from his wounds. In its
place, hay sprouted out of the punctures. Tommy
finally vomited. Nothing came out, though.

"M-Mom?" he asked, his throat parched, his voice
barely above a whisper. "Mom?"

He meant to call louder, but an obstruction
lodged in his constricting throat. Tommy coughed
and hacked.

No words came out. Only hay.

And Harold—now inexplicably in front of
Tommy—stared.

Tommy wrapped his arms around his midsection
and took off for the corn rows. Unripened cobs
battered his face. Serrated leaves cut his skin. He
became vaguely aware of an ominous shadow settling
above him, like the one that enveloped the barn.

Tommy was no writer. No poet. Not like what's-
her-name. But as he wheezed for air and tasted

naught but straw on his tongue, Tommy felt like one
of those dolls whose arms and legs move at the tug of
a string. A doll manipulated by the darkest of hands.

Barreling out of the stalks, Tommy saw his home
scant yards away. He clutched at his insides, unable
to give sound to the agony he felt under his flesh,
and powered forward. His eyes, now spent of tears,
felt dry. But still they went round at the sight of hay
spilling from his sleeves and the cuffs of his jeans.
More and more straw shot from his injuries, from
the itchy and shredded tissues lining his nostrils,
ears, and throat. Even Tommy's skin, once supple and
sun-kissed from mornings spent toiling on the farm,
turned coarse. His flesh took on the aspect of burlap,
and his muscles and bones sublimated into dust.

Tommy Milner crumpled onto the earth just shy
of his family's farmhouse. He tried to scream, but it
came out muffled by the fistfuls of hay now wadded
into his overstuffed husk. With his last iota of consciousness, he swiveled his swollen head about and
saw the scarecrow.

And Harold stared.

No.

Harold smiled.

The Big Toe

sho...
she sa...
for supp...
That...
pieces...
the id...
The...
middle...
voice and it...
"Who took...
August I got...
doesn't know...
he heard the...
"Who took...
The boy pul...
closed his eyes...
I wake up it will be gon...
But soon he heard th...
he heard the... Then the...
"Who took my toe?"
Then the boy heard footsteps move...
kitchen into the dining room, into th...
into the front hall. Then slowly they cl...
stairs.

37

August Hilderbrandt always assumed human flesh would be an acquired taste. Boy, was he wrong. Then again, Auggie didn't know a lot of things, even if he *thought* he did.

His stomach rumbled so loudly, it drowned out the static hiss of Auggie's walkie-talkie on the kitchen table. In truth, he'd been starving since yesterday. Other kids used to tease him about being a picky eater, but Auggie maintained that was born with a refined palate. So, what was someone like Auggie supposed to do? Split some paltry PB and J with a classmate? Eat preservative-filled pasta straight out of the can? Spray processed cheese directly into his mouth?

When he and his friends went out trick-or-treating last night, Auggie figured he'd at least get an apple at one of the homes (no way was he going to eat any of that disgusting penny candy). But this, too, was another example of Auggie being mistaken about something. For he, Chuck, and Stella had been so hungry for revenge, they miscalculated how the rest of their Halloween would unfold. Of course, Auggie imagined himself to be above such base instincts as vengeance. Even at fifteen years of age, he considered himself a sophisticate. Why, Auggie had even dressed as a seventeenth-century character from commedia dell'arte.

But when he saw Tommy Milner's Pontiac Catalina prowl around that corner in Mill Valley, all pretenses of maturity quickly left Auggie. He and his friends immediately opened fire, hurling eggs at the bully's prized automobile. Each yolky splat against the windshield felt like a little victory. Each crunch of eggshell against the hood made up, in some way, for the many recess beatings he had received at Tommy Milner's brutal, corn-fed hands.

Eggs, Auggie thought, his mind returning to the present with another pang of hunger. *I'll poach some eggs...*

He opened the refrigerator, flooding the Hilderbrandts' darkening kitchen with faint yellow light. The ceramic egg carton was empty, as were the rest of the fridge's shelves and drawers. Only a lonely, expired box of baking soda greeted him.

This shouldn't have surprised Auggie. The refrigerator had been empty last night, after he'd returned from the evening's excitement. And it had been empty again in the morning when he woke up and scrounged for breakfast. Come to think of it, the only meal Auggie had eaten in the past twenty-four hours was the meager lunch he bought at the school cafeteria (but he refused to eat the main course: hot dogs). No wonder he was famished.

Auggie began rummaging through the cupboards for some crackers, a tin of anchovies, *anything.* His stomach rumbled louder, and he decided to give his mother a piece of his mind. It was the responsible thing to do, after all. So, Auggie went to the phone on the kitchen wall. His mom had not thought to leave her number on, say, a note affixed to the refrigerator by a magnet, like most mothers might. No, Auggie knew the digits by heart, having dialed them so, so many times in the past.

He went back to rifling through the cupboards, the phone's receiver cradled between his shoulder and ear, its long coil of a cord stretching across the kitchen. The sound of ringing drowned out the crackle of the walkie-talkie on the table. And another gurgle from Auggie's belly.

"Good evening, Hotel Florida," answered a voice. "How may I direct your call?"

Auggie rolled his eyes at the way the receptionist said the hotel's name. *Flo-reed-ah.* As if it were somewhere exotic. But Auggie knew the place

all too well. It was little more than a motel with
a pool and a tiki bar right off the Pennsylvania
turnpike.

"Mrs. Hilderbrandt's room, please," Auggie said
into the phone.

"I'm sorry, I don't see a guest under that name in
our registry," said the receptionist.

Auggie rolled his eyes again, this time more
at his slip of the tongue, and said, "Sorry, Mrs.
Mahaffey's room, please."

"One moment," chimed the receptionist.

A series of connective clicks sounded on the
line, and Auggie finally found a box of cereal in
the cupboard. He gave the cardboard a shake. It was
empty too.

"Hello?" Auggie's mom said over the phone.

"There's nothing here," Auggie began without
greeting or preamble. "The least you could've done
was go to the store before you and Jeff took off
for the weekend..."

"Oh, sorry, Auggie, didn't we?" his mom replied in
a voice strangely devoid of apology. "Must've slipped
my mind in all the hurry to pack. But you know I'd
appreciate it if you stopped calling my husband
by his first name, don't you, Auggie? Can't you just
call Jeff Da—"

"No, I am not gonna call him Dad," Auggie
interrupted.

He heard his mom sigh, and what sounded like
calypso music playing in the background. Despite
his best efforts, Auggie imagined his mom doing the
hula by a motel pool, where passing truckers could
ogle at her in her bikini. He felt a hot flush of
embarrassment followed by the gurgling clamor of
his empty stomach.

"Listen, the limbo line's starting up," Auggie's

mom said. "Jeff Mahaffey's been very good to us. You should be thanking your lucky stars that he's your dad now. I don't understand why you have to call and complain to me—and try to ruin my vacation. I'm sure there's something you can eat."

Auggie crossed the kitchen, opened the refrigerator, and discovered a gleaming pot of stew inside, right next to the box of stale baking soda.

How did I miss that? thought Auggie.

He could've sworn the fridge had been empty only moments ago, just as it was in the morning, and the night before that. Although, Auggie had felt slightly out of sorts—a bit distracted, even—after the little Halloween adventure he'd shared with his friends. Once Chuck had tossed his flaming bag into the Pontiac, Tommy hounded them from the drive-in all the way to the old Bellows place at the edge of Mill Valley. They'd all experienced a few scares along the way. Chuck getting lost on the derelict manse's second story, Tommy locking them all in the cellar, Stella finding that ridiculous book full of fairy tales meant to frighten children . . .

Even Ruth shrieked when she stumbled into all of those cobwebs after getting trapped down there along with the rest of them. Auggie thought it was rather gallant the way he swiped that errant spider off of Ruth's cheek. She thanked him and, in her gratitude, even complimented him on his Pierrot costume. Unlike Chuck and Stella and the rest of Auggie's peers, Ruth was clearly worldly, more cultured. She was even starring in their school's production of *Bye Bye Birdie*. And Auggie had always been tall for his age and mistaken for older.

Maybe Ruth might like to join me for dinner, Auggie now thought. *Maybe Chuck can put in a good word for me. I mean, I am his best friend, and she's his big sister. And maybe Stella's right about Tommy disappearing, and I'll have a shot with Ruth and—*

"August?" his mom repeated over the receiver wedged under his ear.

Her voice dragged Auggie out of his romantic reverie and back to his current starvation.

"I'm eating the stew," he said into the phone. "I'll see you when you get home."

Then Auggie's attention locked on the light bulb in the refrigerator. He watched it glow brighter before spontaneously burning out. The kitchen plunged into darkness, and Auggie became aware of just how late the hour had grown.

Well past dinnertime, he thought.

He flicked the bulb, which sputtered, then returned his attention to the stew. Auggie hung up the phone on the wall, hauled the pot out of the refrigerator, and settled it on the counter. Even in the gloom, the stew looked sumptuous. A velveteen gloss shimmered across its surface from the rendered fats. Whole chunks of root vegetables sat suspended in thick, creamy folds, the consistency looking all the richer from how the roux mingled with the broth. And although Auggie struggled to identify the braised meat, it was so tender that it barely clung to the narrow bones. He inhaled deeply and smelled garlic, aromatics such as rosemary and thyme, and something else—something Auggie could not place, but that was redolent of a familiar, earthy flavor. Grabbing a spoon from the drawer, he prepared to dig in, his mouth salivating like a dog's, when—

"You gotta pick up," squawked the walkie-talkie on the table.

Auggie left the channel open at night in case his friends ever wanted to chat. But on this night, he didn't want to speak with Stella. He just wanted to fill his gut. He wanted to feast.

"Hey, I'm eating," Auggie said into the walkie-talkie.

He released the call button and marveled at the stew again. Something round and plump—a fingerling potato, no doubt—bobbed to the surface. From that point on, Auggie felt pure animal instinct take over. He dunked his spoon into the pot and fed the stew into his mouth, fat potato and all. Auggie had braced himself for the spoonful to be cold, yet he groaned with delight. The stew felt miraculously warm in his mouth. It was the perfect temperature. Normally, Auggie considered most soups and chowders to be rather pedestrian. But this . . . this was delectable. Otherworldly.

His groan continued as he savored the luxurious meaty taste. He chewed into the potato and reacted with only mild surprise as his teeth clamped down on a tough bit. Auggie shrugged and retrieved a small segment of cartilage from between his lips. He put it aside, then spotted another piece of meat floating in the stew and plucked it out.

"Auggie!" Stella's voice warbled over the walkie-talkie again.

He popped the morsel into his mouth, licked his fingers, and, with mounting annoyance, said, "Stella!"

"Don't eat anything!" she cried over the radio waves.

Ignoring her, Auggie probed the stew for more meat while still chewing on the succulent, sinewy strand he'd just ingested. As his spoon scraped against the enameled bottom of the cast iron pot, he failed to notice the kitchen grow darker still. It was as if a shadow, oddly female in shape, extended its arms and flowing locks along the ceiling, making it a black pool, one that consumed all light.

Auggie finally swallowed and answered into the walkie-talkie, "Why? I'm hungry."

Which was true. He continued to ladle spoonful after spoonful of delicious stew into his mouth, gulping down the dense potage. Yet Auggie still felt as if he hadn't eaten in days.

"You're in the next story," Stella's voice said through static. "Listen to me. Do not eat the stew."

Auggie stopped midswallow, looked down at the brimming stewpot on the counter, and thought, *How could she know that I'm eating stew?*

A voracious urge compelled Auggie to take another bite. As his jaws chewed on another hunk of meat, his mind chewed on Stella's warning. And in a bolt of insight, the truth suddenly hit Auggie. He pressed down on the call button again and said, "Har, har. Very funny. Did Chuck put you up to this?"

Auggie pulled himself away from the stew long enough to check out the kitchen window for any sign of his practical joker of a pal, Chuck Steinberg. Dusk had settled throughout the neighborhood. If Chuck was out there, he was laughing at his own antics in the dark. The walkie-talkie in Auggie's hand then broadcast another person's voice—a young man's voice.

"Auggie, this isn't a joke," said the speaker. "The story is writing itself right now."

With another roll of his eyes, Auggie sucked at his own teeth, trying to pry loose a piece of gristle that had gotten lodged. He recognized the speaker at the other end of the frequency. It was that new guy in town, Ramón.

Figures Stella's with him, Auggie thought pointedly. *Girls always fall for the mysterious guys. The ones with the cool cars, the cool hair.*

It wasn't that Auggie didn't like Ramón. They'd only met the night before, and the newcomer had protected Auggie and his friends from Tommy Milner when others had not. Even when Tommy locked all of them in the cellar beneath the Bellows estate, Ramón

had kept his calm. Not even that musty old tome
Stella found in Sarah Bellows's dungeon of a bedroom seemed to rattle him. And now here Ramón was,
humoring Stella once more and talking about that
damn book again. So, no, it wasn't that Auggie didn't
like Ramón. He just resented the way Stella looked
at Ramón after only one night. The way Ruth used to
look at Tommy. The way Auggie's dad used to look at
his mom . . .

"I don't know how. Or why," Ramón continued. "But
I'm reading it right now. 'A sound scared him. It was
a voice, and it called out, "Who took my toe?"'"

"I . . . I know this story," Auggie said absently,
more to himself than to the other end of the walkie-talkie. "My dad used to tell me this story . . ."

Auggie looked around his kitchen again, suddenly feeling self-conscious. He strained to listen
over the two-way crackle, the rushing blood in his
ears, the low and persistent growl of his insatia-
ble intestines. But Auggie heard nothing more. Aside
from himself, the house was empty.

"Am I not supposed to wait for someone to say
that?" Auggie asked in a thick voice, not wanting his
friends to best him with their little game. "'Cause I
don't hear anything."

Despite the comfort food in his belly, Auggie
still felt on edge. He slurped down another spoonful of stew and looked around his home. Left. Right.
In front and back. Every direction except straight
up, where more feminine shadows massed and deep-
ened in obscurity.

"We're reading it right here," Stella's voice insisted.
"Then the voice grew louder. 'Who took my toe?'"

Yeah, yeah, yeah, thought Auggie.

He remembered that part of the story, too.
But the nostalgia evaporated just as quickly as
it came, and Auggie felt bitterness curdle his
tongue. The stew that had seemed so warm and so

nourishing now took on a farinaceous, almost undercooked texture.

Standing there alone in his kitchen, his meal for one spoiled, his friends no doubt giggling at the opposite end of the walkie-talkie connection, August Hilderbrandt perceived himself to be more of a clown than he had been on Halloween night. His paranoia rising, he ripped open the blinds, half expecting to see Chuck on the other side of the glass holding a flaming bag with Auggie's name on it.

But all Auggie saw was his own dumbfounded reflection. His hunger winning out, Auggie splashed the spoon back into the pot and gorged on more stew. His house was vacant, his family was scattered and long gone, but his stomach would be full.

"I'm all alone," Auggie said with his mouth full. "There's no voice..."

He felt a scratchy sensation against his gums. As he hooked his finger into his mouth to fish out the irritant, Stella's crackling voice said, "There has to be a—"

"You are the only one saying it!" Auggie shouted into the walkie-talkie.

It took a few tries, but his saliva-slicked fingers finally grabbed ahold of whatever was itching the inside of his mouth. They pulled out a pale, unbelievably long strand of hair. Globules of congealed grease clung to it like yellow pearls on some awful necklace.

"The voice ... it's us," Auggie heard Stella realize from far away.

His chewing slowed with unease. His molars crunched on something unnaturally hard. Once more, Auggie reached into his mouth. And from it, he removed a rotted big toe. A split toenail hung by a swollen, infected cuticle.

Auggie choked in revulsion as his arms flailed
wildly, knocking the cast iron pot off the counter. It
bashed against the kitchen floor, shattering tiles and
splashing stew everywhere. With the darkness swirling
over his head, Auggie looked down at the puddle at
his feet. Little bits of human flesh sat in fatty lumps
on the ground. He saw an ear. An eye.

"Oh, God," Auggie gagged.

He desperately wanted to regurgitate what he'd
unwittingly devoured. But his stomach was an empty,
wet sack that shuddered with hunger once again.
Auggie ran to the sink and turned on the faucet.
He gargled and spat out sloppy mouthfuls of water,
trying to cleanse himself. But the putrid, mealy taste
remained as sharp as ever. Overcome with violent ill-
ness, Auggie shut off the tap and listened again.

Then he heard it. A voice.

But not from the walkie-talkie. It came from
everywhere and nowhere. From the ceiling. From the
soup pot. From his own quivering guts.

It was getting closer.

"Auggie?" Ramón called over the walkie-talkie.
"Auggie!"

Ramón's voice cut in and out. Either the signal
had grown weak or the batteries. Or perhaps it was
Auggie who had grown weak. His legs became blanched
noodles. His arms hung heavily at his sides, two useless sausages. He couldn't tell if this stupor was the
result of eating too much or still feeling famished.

Auggie staggered back to the counter, gripped the
walkie-talkie in his trembling hand, and said, "Do
you hear that?"

"Hear what?" Ramón responded. "I don't hear—"

"She's telling me a story," Auggie interjected.
"Can you hear that?"

His head started spinning. Everything grew dim.
Auggie wasn't sure if he had held down the call button to talk or not.

"I can't hear you," Ramón's voice said over the fading frequency. "We can't talk at the same time."

Auggie had been depressing the button at the wrong time. He took some small satisfaction in this knowledge, in even being aware of such knowledge while his tainted body turned against him. As he slumped against the kitchen counter and slid down to the stained floor.

"What happens next?" Auggie heard himself say into the walkie-talkie, the tremble spreading from his hands to the rest of his body.

A voice commandeered the radio waves this time, reciting, "August got very scared. But he thought, it doesn't know where I am. It'll never find me..."

"How does the book know that!" Auggie screamed.

Gone were any pretenses of maturity beyond his years. August Hilderbrandt had become little Auggie again, cowering in the mess he'd made on the kitchen floor.

"Then he heard the voice again." Stella was back on the radio, reading from the book from the Bellows's basement.

A wet voice whispered behind Auggie: "Who ... took ... my ... big ... toe?"

He jolted in place behind the counter. Whether Stella or Ramón had heard that, he did not know. All that mattered to him in the moment was that *he* had heard it. And it sounded like it came from the other side of the counter.

Taking a deep breath, focusing through his nausea, Auggie leapt to his feet and bolted out of the kitchen and through the house. His shoes slipped on the oily stew and tender bites of cannibalized skin and muscle. Auggie's long legs kept their balance, but he dropped the walkie-talkie. He hesitated for the briefest of moments about whether

to go back for his only means of communication.
He concluded it was not and ran for the stairs.
He took the steps two at a time and heard Stella's
voice pleading over the static behind him, "Auggie?
Get out!" But that wasn't an option. That ... presence he heard in the kitchen stood between him and
the front door out of the kitchen. So Auggie's only
recourse was to scramble up to the second story and
barricade himself until help arrived.

Surely Stella will come, Auggie thought in
desperation. *Her place is only a couple of blocks
away. She'll bring Ramón. And her dad. I'll even settle for Chuck!*

Reaching the landing at the top of the stairs,
he looked up and down the hallway, finding no one.
Auggie ran into his bedroom, trailing soupy footprints as he went. Just
before he slammed the door
shut, he looked back over
his shoulder.

A corpse now stood at
the end of the hall, its
hideous, lurching body
barely visible in the
shrinking space between
the closing door and
the jamb.

Auggie backed
away from his door,
tiptoeing across
his neat, orderly
room. Slivers of
moonlight played
against the walls,
leaving bright
slashes on the
various theater and travel

49

posters his father had bought him ages ago.

Ice ran down Auggie's spine when he heard a floorboard shift in the hall.

Creak.

Auggie eased himself onto the ground, careful not to breathe, and shimmied his long, lean form under his bed.

Creak.

That footstep was closer. Auggie bit his tongue so hard he drew blood. It tasted almost as coppery as the delicious stew.

cREAK.

The shadows of two feet crossed the open slit between Auggie's bedroom door and the floor. He froze in place.

"Who ... took ... my ... toe?" called the voice.

Auggie silently cursed as the doorknob began to turn. A decomposing right foot stepped into the bedroom. The left foot dragged after the right. And its big toe was missing.

Creak. Right.

Auggie covered his mouth with his hand, stifling a sob.

Creak. Left.

Auggie's body wracked silently under the bed. But he dared not make a sound.

Creak. Right.

This thing that had been trailing Auggie for so long—this nagging that left him feeling unsatisfied and alone at every meal—had finally caught up with Auggie. The cadaver's mutilated feet stood right in front of his face. Black liquid oozed from the open wound where the big toe had been. Auggie clenched his eyes shut, squeezing out tears. And when they reopened, they saw that the space at the foot of the bed... was empty.

Baffled, Auggie blinked. The nine toes were gone. So was the livid gore that had seeped out of the missing toe's stump. Remembering to breathe again, Auggie slowly crawled partway out from beneath the bed frame. Dust bunnies tickled his nose and adhered to the sweat running down his face and neck. He glanced upward and saw that his room and his bed were completely, mercifully empty.

Then two chopped hands clamped around his ankles. Auggie felt himself yanked back under the bed. His body rigid with fear, he felt strained, soggy respiration blow against his cheek. It reeked of garbage. Of ruined meat. Of the maggots that dined upon it.

Auggie craned his head to the side and saw the grotesque, pitiless face of the corpse beside him. Hair fell in clumps off its torn and peeling scalp. Worms milled in the spaces between its remaining teeth. And two suppurating gouges glared back at Auggie in place of the eyes they'd once contained. Auggie wondered whether that big toe had been the only body part he'd had inadvertently enjoyed.

The carcass wrenched open its jaws with a loud

click. Bile dribbled out of what passed for its lips.
And August Hilderbrandt realized he was about to
hear the end of the scary story that had come back
to haunt him.

"Boooooo!" shrieked the corpse.

Once more, Auggie experienced an aggressive tug on his legs. He screamed as he was pulled further under the bed. Auggie clawed at the floor, trying to stop his backward slide. His fingernails scored the varnish, leaving erratic scratches before tearing loose from Auggie's raw nail beds. The retreating sight of his broken nails wedged in the floorboards made Auggie think of the nail that hung so tremulously from that big toe—that big toe that had tasted so damn good.

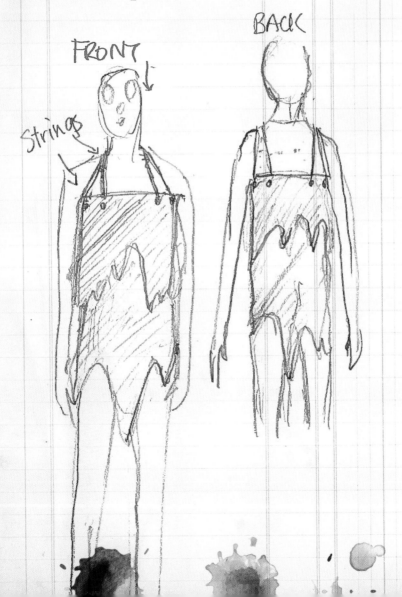

The Red Spot

a crazy
mot

57

Ruth Steinberg overheard the gossip and wanted to scream. It wouldn't have been her first scream that week. And given the throbbing pain in the left half of her face, it likely wouldn't be her last.

She turned in her chair, purposefully aiming her right side—her good side—at the chatty actresses across the dressing room, and glared at them. They abruptly stopped gossiping and averted their eyes, going back to applying makeup and costumes. Ruth's painted lips pursed in satisfaction. It was the closest she could get to making a smile with the current tautness of her skin. But looking back at the lit vanity mirror in front of her, Ruth's grin faded.

Because the reflection showed both Ruth's good side and her bad side.

Not that Ruth had a bad side. Not normally, anyway. Of course, Ruth would be the first to tell her many, many, many friends that she was far from perfect. For one thing, she had an annoying little brother, Chuck. And for another, Ruth had to work at least twice as hard as the other talented performers in *Bye Bye Birdie* to memorize her lines and be the absolute best actress on the stage. Yes, the truth was, it wasn't easy being Ruth Steinberg. And it wasn't even her fault.

She was born this way. Ruth was born pretty.

"Did you see it?"

"What's on her face?"

Ruth heard her costars whispering about her again. Despite herself, she shrunk down in her chair. The bulbs around the vanity mirror cast her left cheek in stark relief, even though she had unpinned her blonde hair in an attempt to cover it. Ruth felt her blood start to simmer.

So what? So what if the other girls had nothing better to do than fixate on her? So what if Ruth had a blemish on her face? It was just a pimple.

It was just a red spot.

"She's not actually going out on stage, is she?"

"Disgusting..."

Ruth ignored the hushed, tittering voices in the dressing room and applied more concealer to her cheek. Of course, the other girls wouldn't understand. Couldn't understand. And for once, Ruth almost envied *them*.

Why, some days, Ruth almost wished that she were like those other girls—that she wasn't so good-looking. She occasionally wondered what it would feel like to be free of that burden and trade places with one of the ordinary, unremarkable students in her school. Like Chuck's little friend Stella. There was a plain Jane if Ruth ever saw one.

Then again, Ruth felt that she also had a responsibility to the good people of Mill Valley to use her looks in a positive way. It'd be a sin to not take advantage of a God-given gift, right?

So, when all the boys would follow Ruth and buy her malts at the drugstore and give her their letterman jackets when she got cold, Ruth gladly accepted their attentions. She even accepted the attentions of a few of the ladies around her, although those stares were of a different sort.

Long before Ruth turned seventeen, she became aware of the jealousy directed at her. Even grown women seemed to resent Ruth's beauty. Well, not Ruth's mom. Mrs. Steinberg hardly ever commented on her daughter's appearance. She was always too busy fawning over Chuck, making him snacks and sewing stupid Halloween costumes for him. Ruth didn't get any help with her wardrobe for *Bye Bye Birdie*, naturally, and had to make it herself thank-you-very-much. But she didn't care about that, just like she didn't care about the envious scowls she received on a daily basis.

Take the mother of Chuck's other little
friend, Auggie, for example. Ruth would feel Mrs.
Hilderbrandt's eyes on her whenever the middle-aged
woman dropped off her son at Mill Valley High. And
each and every time, Ruth new exactly what Mrs.
Hilderbrandt was thinking.

*I used to look that way. I used to be young. I
used to beautiful.*

But Ruth never let on that she knew what she
knew. Why should she? It wasn't her fault. She was
born this way. Ruth was born pretty. She was going
to live pretty. And by God, if Ruth had anything to
say about it, she was going to die pretty, too, with
a little help from Avon, some Aqua Net, and a whole
lot of positive thinking.

Mrs. Steinberg once told her daughter (this was
before Chuck came along, obviously) something she'd
read in a self-help book. According to this book, suc-
cessful people envision their accomplishments before
they happen. They form a picture in their heads of
what they want and—*poof!*—they will it into being.

Ruth shut her eyes in the dressing room and
imagined the ovation she'd receive after her
star-making turn in the school play. It was going to
be a standing ovation, actually. Everyone would be
cheering and clapping, and Tommy would walk over
from the wings with a gorgeous bouquet of lilies
and—well, no, not Tommy, because he had just gone
missing, and good riddance to that creep. But some
other cute guy would fight off the rest to give Ruth
her flowers and then take her to dinner. Like, actually take her to dinner, instead of just saying he
was going to take her to dinner and then driving
them to the make-out section of the drive-in instead.
And at this dinner, Ruth could order anything she
wanted (even the lobster, because he would insist).

And people would keep coming up to Ruth and her
new beau, and they'd apologize for interrupting, but
they just *had* to say something to Ruth. They had to
tell her how fabulous she looked onstage, sure, but
also how much her performance had moved them.

With a contented sigh, Ruth opened her eyes.
She finished dusting her cheek with powder and
appraised her reflection once more. *There.* No one in
the audience would be able to tell Ruth had a zit.

Another actress sat beside Ruth, looked into
their shared mirror, and flinched. She pointed at
the red spot and said, "Oh, honey, you need to do
something about that."

The girls around them didn't even bother to
cover their smirks or giggles. Ruth felt the boil on
her cheek pulsate even harder. Seething with anger
and unaccustomed to this strange sense of humilia-
tion, she pushed past her fellow actresses (support-
ing players, really).

Ruth went to the restroom. Her heels clicked a
strident beat down the school's hallway. She passed
a banner that read, "Mill Valley High Proudly
Presents 'Bye Bye Birdie' Nov. 2nd-8th" and resisted
the impulse to snatch it down and tear it apart with
her bare hands. But that would ruin Ruth's manicure,
and she was not about to do that. Ruth already had
to cake a ton of foundation on her face and undo
her normal bouffant to veil that red spot. Enough
was enough already.

She opened the ladies' room door and found a
bunch of loud girls inside. They instantly stopped
chattering and gaped back at Ruth's face with wide,
disbelieving eyes. Ruth spun around and marched off
toward another restroom. As she went, she caught
snippets of the girls' remarks through the closing
bathroom door.

"Gross."

"What's with the fright makeup?"

"Doesn't she know Halloween's over?"

Halloween. That's when all of this trouble started
for Ruth in the first place. As she rushed up a
staircase, she thought back to two nights prior.
Tommy Milner had offered to buy her dinner (surprise, surprise). Ruth had her doubts about his true
intentions by then, but what else was she supposed
to do? Go out trick-or-treating with Chuck and his
nerdy friends? That was baby stuff. Besides, chocolate made Ruth's skin break out.

But the night went off course sooner than
expected when Tommy decided to steal candy from
kids instead. Ruth hinted that Tommy should stop,
but he was already drunk. And honestly? Tommy
looked positively handsome when he acted mischie-
vously. So, Tommy and his pals had their fun, and
Ruth was about to get her long-awaited dinner, when
none other than Chuck lit a brown paper bag on fire
and tossed it into Tommy's Pontiac.

Ruth had seen her little brother angling in their
toilet with a fish net, so she already knew what was
inside the bag before Tommy accidentally smeared it
all over himself. Seeing another perfectly good evening dashed, Ruth was ready to call it quits.

Only, Tommy got that wild look in his eye. He
could be a mean drunk. She had seen how he treated
that pathetic scarecrow on his family's farm. So
her irritation turned to concern when she realized
Tommy wanted to treat her kid brother the same way.

Reaching the top of the steps, Ruth hurried down
the corridor to the school's second-floor restrooms,
the blister on her cheek stinging worse than before.
Her pink stage costume swished back and forth as
she went, and Ruth suddenly became concerned with
the time. She spotted a clock on the wall above
a bank of lockers. Ten minutes until curtains up.

Plenty of time to do what needed to be done.

Just like Ruth did what needed to be done on Halloween. She had pleaded with Tommy to let bygones be bygones, but he was far past listening. He dragged Ruth with him all the way to that filthy Bellows place at the edge of town. Ruth never liked to frown (it causes lines around the eyes and mouth). But when Tommy trapped Chuck and his friends in the cellar, she had to put her foot down.

And what did Ruth get for standing up for others? Tommy shoved her into the basement with the rest. He even called her "trash" before locking the door on the lot of them.

Trash? Ruth knew who the real trash was, and it was Tommy Milner. She supposed the fashionable thing to do would be to feign worry now that Tommy was missing. But he didn't deserve her worry, the same as how he didn't deserve her. He probably wasn't even missing. Chief Turner should have started by checking all the bars in Mill Valley.

Ruth's staccato footsteps echoed along the hallway, until she reached the second-story ladies' room. Shutting her eyes, she imagined it was empty, and opened the door. *Poof!* A vacant bathroom awaited Ruth. She hummed in singsong approval and went to the mirror.

Ruth gasped. The red spot, little more than a bump mere moments ago, had ballooned into an enormous welt. Its base flared red, while the tight skin along the mound looked white and shiny. The clogged pore had gotten so large and infected, it made Ruth's entire face seem lopsided. She couldn't even open her left eye as wide as the right because her cheek pushed up against her lower lid.

There was no imagining this away, Ruth realized. She touched the boil and winced in pain. Ruth then turned on the hot-water faucet and hoped the steam would loosen the obstruction. As she bent over to dab some warm water onto her face, she almost thought she saw a shadow shift in the mirror. But that was probably just the glass fogging over.

Standing upright again, Ruth braced herself against the basin. She was about to rub the condensation off the mirror when she heard a whisper, this one lower and raspier than that of the other girls.

Ruth slowly turned around. Maybe the bathroom wasn't quite as empty as she had believed. But a quick peek under all the stall doors confirmed Ruth was alone in there. That faint voice must have been a figment of her powerful imagination. As loath as Ruth was to admit it, people's whispers did affect her. They lingered and they hurt her feelings. Especially when they were true.

Her hand squeaked against the mirror as she finally wiped the film of steam off of it. On the other side of the glass, another woman's disfigured reflection stared back at Ruth.

Ruth screamed in horror. She twirled around again, expecting that ghastly figure to be standing right behind her. But no one was there.

After several seconds of not breathing, Ruth felt her heart beat again. Blood coursed through her veins, palpating that abhorrent pimple with a steady rhythm.

It had to be the stress cracking Ruth up, turning her imagination against her and ruining her normally pristine complexion. She remembered reading in another one of her mother's self-help books (Mrs. Steinberg would have been too busy fussing over Chuck at this point to dote on her daughter) how stress could take a toll on one's body and mind. Anyone could see that the stress of Halloween night had triggered Ruth's breakout. And the stress of memorizing all those lines—basically carrying the

entire production of *Bye Bye Birdie* all by herself—
only compounded that blemish. It made her see things
that weren't there.

But there was one thing that really was there.
One thing that was the source of all of Ruth
Steinberg's recent woes.

The zit had to go.

Ruth leaned closer to the mirror, its surface no
longer fogged, and eyed the lump on her cheek. She
could almost see it thrum in time with her pulse. She
could almost see something ... *wriggle* just beneath
the stretched surface.

With her gaze so focused on her blighted visage,
Ruth failed to notice the shadows around her start
to move. They, too, wriggled, like the matching arms
of some half-dead bug. The shadows spread in tan-
dem, unfurling up the walls and across the ceiling.
The dark lines intersected and wove together into a
black web. But Ruth just couldn't pull her eyes away
from the growth on her face. The shadows dripped
back down the walls, and again, something moved
beneath her skin. Ruth clenched her jaws in agony,
and the strain forced a short, ingrown hair to poke
out of the pimple.

Ruth whimpered. How could her body—which everyone loved, by the way—produce something so unbelievably unsightly? What had Ruth ever done to
deserve such embarrassment, and on opening night,
no less? Hadn't she always been generous to her
followers? Hadn't she always acted the model citizen
in "quaint" Mill Valley? Ruth was going to put this
Podunk town on the map just as soon as she got discovered in Hollywood. Just as soon as she stole the
show in *Bye Bye Birdie.*

Just as soon as she popped this goddamn zit.

Ruth tugged on the freed hair, but it didn't budge.
Gritting her teeth for the sting to come, she reached
for the coarse whisker again. But before Ruth could

touch it, the hair twitched. Like it was alive.

Stifling another whimper, Ruth leaned even closer to the mirror. She scrutinized the ingrown hair and now saw that it wasn't a hair at all.

It was a little leg.

It bent at the joint, and again Ruth screamed She cupped her hands over the enlarging red spot and felt something spilling against her trembling fingers. Ruth assumed the bump had ruptured and that she'd now have to clean up the pus that wept into her palms—and fast, before her first number started. Maybe she could run down to the girls' locker room and find some toothpaste. That was supposed to help with acne, wasn't it?

Ruth visualized her action plan in her head. She was going to do this. She was going to make her cue and dazzle all those jealous jerks in the cheap seats. She was going to ignore the weird tickling sensation under her hands.

Ruth's body went limp with dread. Her fingers couldn't so much as make a fist. They parted. And from the spaces between them, dozens of baby spiders escaped across Ruth's face.

She screamed louder than she ever had at any audition. She pulled her hands away. An endless stream of arachnids spread from the punctured flap of skin that used to be her cheek.

An animal panic overcame Ruth. She clawed at the hatching spiders, scoring her flesh with her polished nails and drawing even more blood. But her spastic swatting only seemed to hasten the arrival of more of them.

The skein of shadows around Ruth constricted until the only light in Mill Valley High's second-story girls' room went out. Ruth didn't scream this time so much as wail in raw, abject terror. She felt

the last of the air leave her lungs and perceived a
new darkness stitch itself together over her eyes. It
was blacker than the shadows that befell her.

Ruth backed into the corner and dropped to her
knees, skinning them and ripping the hem of her
dress—her dress that she made because no one else
wanted to. Not even her own mother. With a wracking
sob, Ruth curled into the fetal position. She writhed
and shrieked in the corner, more and more spiders
coating her body in a blanket equal parts liquid
and abrasive.

Was this what Tommy wanted when he hurled Ruth
into that bug-infested cellar? Was this what all
the other girls wanted to see—Ruth Steinberg pro-
faned and suffering on the ground? Oh, that was
always the way, wasn't it? People loved to put someone special on a pedestal before shoving them back
down to the dirt, especially the hillbillies in Mill
Valley. Especially Chuck. That little bastard would
be laughing about this forever, and Mrs. Steinberg
wouldn't ever tell him to stop. Not her little boy.
Not the apple of her eye. Not her favorite child.

Ruth suddenly felt a sudsy splash against her
head. Eyes no longer blindfolded by thousands of
pinching legs, she looked up and saw who soaked her.

It was Chuck.

He dropped the janitor's mop bucket and ran to
his sister's side. Behind him, Chuck's friend Stella
stood paralyzed in shock, while some other boy
doffed his leather jacket and slapped it against the
fleeing spiders.

Ruth was vaguely aware that Chuck was saying something to her, even as light returned to
the bathroom. In the buzzing glow of the florescent bulbs, Ruth saw a crowd of rubberneckers at
the open restroom door—and countless spider bites
along every square inch of her exposed flesh. A con-
stellation of inflamed little red spots.

"It's okay, you're going to be okay," Ruth heard Chuck say.

Her eyes fluttered, and her numb hands swiped at the spiders that were no longer on her face. With a distant and confused gaze, she said, "She was here ... I saw her ... the light ... crawling ... the spiders. They are all over me ..."

"They're all gone now, Ruthie," Chuck said to her as if she were the younger sibling, not him. "They're all gone."

But what the hell did he know? Stupid kid. Ruth could feel them. She could still feel them, even if others couldn't see them. They were skittering over and under her skin.

"All over me ... my face ..." Ruth began before becoming more agitated. "Look at me! They came from inside of me. Out of my face. It was my zit."

Chuck, Stella, the cute guy with the leather jacket, and the growing crowd of onlookers all stared at Ruth—not in awe of her beauty but out of pity for what the spiders had exposed. Ruth broke down crying. Between her tears and the scratches on her corneas, she looked past the gathered crowd to the clock on the wall behind them, above a bank of lockers.

It was late. *Bye Bye Birdie* had already begun. And Ruth had missed her big entrance.

The paramedics had to strap Ruth's hands to the
gurney to keep her from clawing at herself. As they
loaded her into the ambulance, she saw her parents
watching tearfully from outside Mill Valley High,
their grief apparent in the flashing red and white
lights. Ruth's mom was looking at her and her alone,
not at Chuck.

A deranged smile spread across Ruth's bloody,
bitten lips. It felt good to smile, especially with
that engorged mass now deflated on her cheek. That
smile became a laugh. And that laugh became a
throaty cackle that pierced louder than the ambulance's siren as it drove away.

The girls in the Mill Valley High drama club
would be gossiping about that cackle for genera-
tions. Ruth Steinberg was finally famous for more
than her looks.

But it wasn't Ruth's fault. She was born that way.
She was born pretty.

The Dream

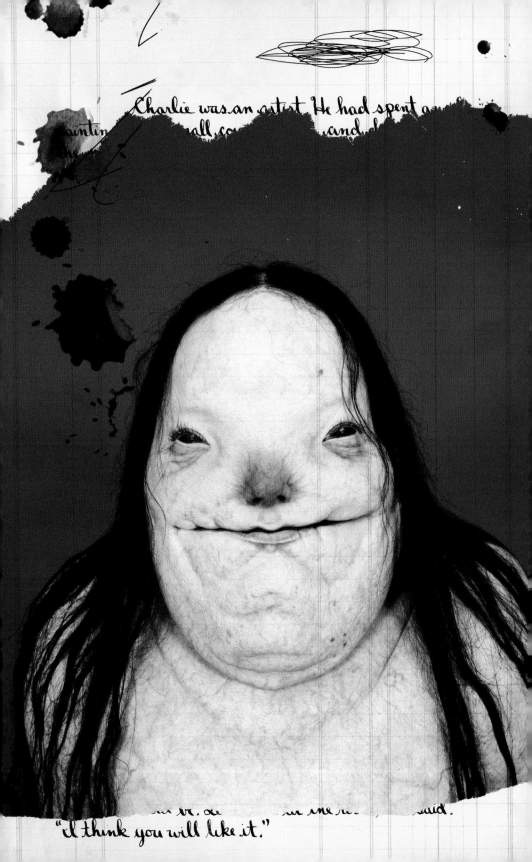

Charlie was an artist. He had spent a... painting... all co... ...and...

"I think you will like it."

Nobody in Chuck's circle was in much of a laughing mood lately. Strange things had been happening in their hometown. Chuck always quipped how he'd love for something exciting to happen in Mill Valley sometime this century. But this wasn't what he had in mind, not even in his most outlandish comedic fantasies.

First, Tommy Milner went missing.

"Hoo, that Tommy Milner, I tell ya," Chuck once riffed during lunch in the school cafeteria. "If you look up the word *bully* in the dictionary, you'll see Tommy's picture—right between *body odor* and *bumbling*!"

Tommy had strutted into the cafeteria right in the middle of the punch line. Tommy beat the shit out of Chuck that day and gave him such a severe wedgie that Chuck groaned he could still taste the "fruit of the loom" weeks later.

But Chuck got the last laugh a few nights ago, on Halloween, when he filled a brown paper bag with his own turd, lit it on fire, and tossed the foul, flaming thing into Tommy's Pontiac Catalina. Now, that was funny. That was the most legendary prank Chuck had ever pulled, even better than the cherry-bomb toilet explosions at Camp Tacony a few summers ago. That was also the last night Chuck—or anyone—had seen Tommy Milner.

Then, one day later, Chuck's best pal, Auggie, also vanished. Auggie had always been the straight man to Chuck's jester. The Martin to his Lewis. The chocolate to Chuck's peanut butter. Chuck would routinely bring Auggie down a peg or two whenever he'd start rambling about some Italian play or dim sum restaurant or whatever. But Auggie never got too sore over the ribbing. Chuck always thought Auggie got a kick out of their banter, like he was saying his comeback lines with a wink.

Auggie may have been a snob, but he was a loyal friend. Numerous times—too many to count—he had pulled Chuck's fat out of the fire. Even as recently as this Halloween, Auggie was there for Chuck. After they and Stella ambushed Tommy Milner's car and Tommy chased them all the way to the old Bellows place, Chuck got separated from his friends inside the foreboding mansion.

Sure, it started as another of Chuck's tricks, only, it turned out that the trick was on him. He decided to play a quick round of surprise hide-and-seek with Auggie. Chuck always loved to tweak Auggie when he was nervous, and the creepy Bellows place was making everyone nervous. So, Chuck snuck to the second floor of the rundown estate and hid in an antique in one of the upstairs bedrooms. He waited for Auggie to walk past obliviously, then opened the door.

Only, when Chuck did, he found that the bedroom was no longer in a shambles but somehow restored to its original, ornate condition. Nor was Chuck alone. An impossibly gaunt old woman in a black lace gown and veil sat in repose along the bed. At the foot of the bed, the meanest black dog Chuck had ever seen stared back at him, as if sizing up Chuck for the kill. The old woman rapped her walking stick against the hardwood floor three times, and Chuck flinched so hard he nearly pissed his pants. He retreated back into the dresser and shut the door. The door started rattling from the outside, and Chuck held on for dear life.

But when Chuck finally lost the tug-of-war and the dresser opened again, it wasn't the hellhound. It was Auggie.

My hero, Chuck mentally deadpanned.

The next night, Auggie disappeared too.

Chuck noticed that losing his best friend had given his latest jokes more of an edge. The setups

grew grimmer, the payoffs sharper and more provoc-
ative. Stella was long past humor at this point, and
Ruth had never suffered her little brother's brand
of "comedy" for the entire time he'd known her.

Now Ruth was gone too.

Chuck startled awake from another dream. He
found himself on a northbound bus. Stella and that
guy they met on Halloween, Ramón, were seated
nearby, leaning against each other and looking out
the window at the passing fields. Chuck saw how
they were holding hands, that damned book from the
Bellows place next to their interwoven fingers.

The very sight of the book's frayed leather binding, its faded endpapers, its bloodred script, made
Chuck's skin crawl. It instantly reminded him of the
nightmare he'd just left. The dream on the bus had
been the same as the last. The pale, plump woman. The
black eyes and tangle of hair. The red room.

Chuck shuddered involuntarily and rubbed the
sleep from his eyes. He noticed that the driver
was slowing. Peering past Stella and Ramón and
through the window, Chuck saw the bus turn onto the
grounds of a sprawling stone structure. They passed
a sign that read "The New Pennhurst Hospital."

For some reason, the sight of the impassive complex and its barred windows made Chuck think of a
nursery rhyme he'd recently heard.

The worms crawl in, the worms crawl out...

Maybe Chuck recalled the song because of the
crazy old lady who had muttered it to him.

The worms play pinochle on your snout...

She seemed like she could've been a former
patient at Pennhurst—one who escaped before the
doctors ever found a cure.

They'll eat your ears, they'll eat your nose,
they'll eat the jelly between your toes...

Of course, the demented woman had never been a

patient at Pennhurst. But it had been her idea that
Stella, Ramón, and Chuck visit the hospital.

Don't ever laugh as the hearse goes by...

Senile though she may have been, the elderly
lady told them that Pennhurst held the answers to
the book they'd found. And to the fates it had foretold, fates that had befallen everyone else who'd
been with them at the Bellows place.

"You may be the next to die..."

The bus came to a stop, its shot brakes releasing
a shrill metal-on-metal squeal that set Chuck's teeth
on edge. He, Stella, and Ramón got off and made
their way to the main building. A thick patina of
overgrown ivy gave the hospital's faҳade an ancient
appearance. It seemed as if it'd been there for cen-
turies, not decades.

And this is the New Pennhurst Hospital? Chuck
thought. *What happened to the old one—it get demol-
ished during the big bang?*

For the hundredth time that day, Chuck wished
his best friend were there to share in the joke.
Chuck knew Stella and Ramon wouldn't laugh at it,
but Auggie would've.

As the trio approached the hospital's main
entrance, Chuck looked off to the distance, past
Pennhurst's vast gables, where the sun had started
its descent. The sky went amber with slanting light,
and purple clouds spread over it like bruises. The
contrast, and the late-afternoon hour, triggered
another connection in Chuck's mind.

"Have you guys noticed how all the stories take
place at night?" Chuck asked his companions. "Tommy.
Auggie. Ruth ... all at night."

Stella and Ramón exchanged a look but said
nothing. And that silence told Chuck everything he
needed to know. He was right. And another night was
fast approaching.

Getting past the battle-ax nurse at the front desk

was a pain in the ass. If Stella had let Chuck do the talking, he could've easily improvised some song and dance, charmed the spinster, and probably gotten the three of them all-access passes. Instead, Stella had to try the mostly honest route. Fat lot of good that did them.

To make matters worse, a passing doctor said how the hospital's records were stored in "the red room." Stella and Ramon's ears perked up: That's where they wanted to go. But Chuck almost wet himself for the second time that week at the sound of those three little words. What were the chances he would've dreamed twice about that bloated old broad warning him to keep away from a red room—only to have some shrink mention an off-limits red room?

Chuck decided that, if he survived this ... whatever this was ... he might try his hand at being a psychic to the stars. He'd wear a turban and a cape, the whole enchilada. All the late-night talk shows would be tripping over themselves to book the Great Chuckini so that he could tell celebrities their fortunes and bend spoons with his mind. Yeah, that's what Chuck would do.

If he survived.

With that new life goal in mind, Chuck reluctantly followed Stella and Ramón as they snuck past the distracted nurse's front desk. Slipping through a set of restricted access doors, the three high schoolers skidded to a halt at the intersection between two antiseptic hallways. A sign on the corner pointed to the left and read: "R.E.D.—Records and Evaluation Department."

Their little search party sighed in collective relief, and Ramón said, "So, it's not actually red. You're fine."

Which was easy for Ramón to say. He wasn't the

one who kept dreaming about pale ladies and weirdo
warnings. Chuck rolled his eyes in aggravation.

"It's called the red room," Chuck countered. "Who
said it had to be red? Count me out!"

"Okay, stay here then," Stella said impatiently.
"We'll be quick. Catch ya later?"

Chuck nodded nervously and said, "Not if ya
catch a disease first."

It was their group's favorite rejoinder, and
saying it gave Chuck's spirits a slight lift. He knew
Stella and Ramón were eager to find the old hospital records of whoever authored the book that had
been cursing them. But Chuck couldn't have cared
less about some musty old medical charts, even
if they were kept in a room that was painted with
bright pink polka dots.

No, Chuck Steinberg had his own reason for
breaking into Pennhurst Hospital.

He watched Stella and Ramón run off toward the
R.E.D. room—which sounded ominous to Chuck even as
an acronym—and dawdled in the crossroads between
hallways for a minute longer, until a pair of
nurses rounded one of the corners.

Chuck tried to act casual, like he owned the joint,
as he turned his back to the oncoming nurses and
walked briskly down one of the perpendicular halls.
He reached an elevator and ducked inside just before
its automatic doors closed. The good news, as near as
Chuck could tell, was that the elevator was empty.
But the bad news? It was headed toward the roof.

After an interminably long upward crawl, the
elevator's undergreased cables straining and squeal-
ing like out-of-tune guitar strings, the doors opened
with the most depressing *ding* Chuck had ever heard.

*Jesus, who handles the repairs at this hospital—
Dr. Frankenstein?* he mused.

Chuck chuckled at his one-liner and stepped onto
the roof, disoriented by the dizzying height and the

sudden chill in the air. He followed a walkway to
the edge of the roof and peered down the side. Far
below on the hospital grounds, two identical albino
patients with matching haunted expressions smiled
back at him. It seemed to Chuck that the brothers
had been looking up to the roof before Chuck even
peeked over the edge. The twins pointed at him in
unison, their rictus smiles unchanging, their hospital gowns as bleached white as their hair. Chuck
took a startled step back.

Shaking off an unexpected case of vertigo, he
heard one of the two rooftop doorways open behind
him. A pair of orderlies—beefy, brawny guys in
bleached and pressed scrubs—walked out, making
their rounds of the premises. Chuck guessed that
some of the inmates (sorry, *patients*) would steal
up here if they could. After all, flinging your-
self off the roof would be one way to check out of
Pennhurst Hospital.

"You know where you're going?" one of the orderlies asked.

Chuck made a quick appraisal and decided that
these guys probably weren't in a mood to hear the
one about the priest, the rabbi, and the man who
claimed he was Queen Victoria. Stalling for time,
Chuck stammered. His eyes flicked to the side. And
then he saw it.

The sunset had turned the sky the deepest shade
of red. Night was near.

And so were the no-nonsense orderlies. Chuck kept
his eyes glued to the ground and made a beeline for
the second rooftop door. He passed through it and
hustled down another hall, the orderlies following
a few paces behind him.

"Hey, you there!" one orderly called after him.
"You're not supposed to be here!"

No shit, Sherlock, thought Chuck.

He rushed around the nearest corner, saw another open elevator (thank you, Dr. Frankenstein!), and hit one of the buttons. But rather than take the ride down, Chuck hopped out of the elevator and into a supply closet on the opposite wall. He eased the door shut and listened as the orderlies reached the elevator, which had just shut and begun its descent. Chuck heard the orderlies gripe on the other side of the closet door and run for the nearest staircase. They actually fell for it. The ol' empty elevator trick.

Suckers! Chuck thought with supreme satisfaction.

Then he took in his cramped surroundings. The supply closet was filled chockablock with wheelchairs in various states of disrepair. And the emergency floodlight overhead made the white-painted walls look stark raving red.

Chuck instinctively ran through every swear word he knew in his head.

So this is it. Trapped like a rat in a red room after all. Son of a ...

Only, it wasn't a red room, Chuck soon realized. At least, not technically. This was a closet, complete with a water heater and a mop bucket and an insane number of wheelchairs. And that deeply disturbing dream lady with the pale skin and the midriff bulge and the black eyes that were too far apart didn't say anything about a closet! She specifically visited his nightmares in a room.

Proud of himself for identifying the loophole in dream logic, Chuck mock dusted his shoulders and flicked the light switch to his side. The overhead bulb went from crimson to florescent white, and Chuck pumped his fist in the air victoriously. He could've kissed whatever lunatic stuffed all those goddamn wheelchairs in there.

Finding one that was still mostly intact, Chuck sat in it. He kicked open the closet door and

wheeled out into the hallway, which was remark-
ably, blessedly white.

"I love white," Chuck said cheerfully to no one in
particular. "White walls, white bread, white clothes..."

He passed an unattended laundry cart filled with,
of all things, freshly washed white hospital coats.
Chuck happily stood up, donned one of the coats,
and then pushed an imaginary patient in the vacant
wheelchair down the corridor. Maybe he was on to
something with this psychic thing!

"White Christmas," Chuck added.

Then, Chuck stopped short. He took a few steps
back and regarded the vending machine he'd just
passed. Chuck wagged his eyebrows, feeling the
much-needed turn his luck was taking, and said,
"White chocolate!"

He patted his pockets and felt a few coins jin-
gling within. After some digging, Chuck fished out
enough and plunked them into the machine. He read
the menu, then punched the code for the whitest
candy bar on display. The metal coil holding the
treat on display started to turn—when the vending
machine's lights flickered out. The bar remained
stuck in place.

"You trash can!" he yelled.

Chuck snaked his arm up through the dispenser
bin and toward the dangling candy, but it was just
beyond his grasp. A frustrating turn of events, to be
sure. But Chuck reasoned that if this turned out to be
the worst thing to happen to him today, he'd still con-
sider himself the most fortunate S.O.B. on the planet.

About to give up, he banged his fist on the cabi-
net. The white chocolate bar fell loose—followed by
three more goodies. Chuck greedily grabbed up his
winnings and tried to calculate how long it'd take
to reach Atlantic City by bus. The Great Chuckini
was liking his odds.

But when he heard some approaching adult voices,
Chuck abandoned the wheelchair and retreated into the
closest bathroom—only after he confirmed its walls
were white too. He took the farthest stall, locked the
door, and started to chow down on his chocolate. Night
loomed beyond the windows, but Chuck couldn't care
less. The sugar rush did wonders for his anxiety. Four
bars later (those doctors loved to talk—didn't they
have any actual patients to visit?), Chuck emerged
from the john and made sure the coast was clear.

Stuffing his hands in his purloined coat's pockets and whistling a carefree tune, he made a left,
then a right, then another left before encountering
a long row of padlocked doors. Chuck had almost
forgotten. In his overriding fear of red rooms, he
nearly neglected his real reason for taking the
long, long bus ride to Pennhurst.

Each door featured a small square window in its
center. The glass contained a grid of strong metal
wires that overlapped in a diamond pattern. Chuck
was already hip to the reason why. A patient could
punch through glass, but not wire.

Chuck braved a glimpse into the first window,
then the next. Both of those cells contained men.
Well, sad heaps that used to be men. Then, Chuck
approached a third door. He knew that comedy worked
in threes. The first time a crowd hears a good joke,
it gets a laugh. The second time, it gets applause.
But on the third time? The joke *kills*.

The Great Chuckini said a prayer, hoped his luck
held, and took a breathless look into the third window. And there she was.

"Ruthie?" Chuck said, his voice almost a whisper.

The figure on the other side of the door stirred,
barely visible in the faint moonlight coming from
the barred skylight set high into the ceiling. Chuck
gently tapped the reinforced glass and said, "Ruth,
it's me. It's Chuck."

The girl inside the cell turned. She had evidently undone the straitjacket that once confined her in the twenty-four hours since she'd been committed to Pennhurst. The loose straps dangled from Ruth Steinberg's body like eight extra appendages.

"I ... I talked to Mom," Chuck added after getting no response from his sister. "She's gonna come visit you just as soon as she can. She's gonna bring the program too. From your show. It's got your name on it, right under '*Bye Bye Birdie*.'"

Ruth moved so fast, Chuck didn't even have time to react. She slammed her whole body against the door. Chuck saw the hinges hold, but the cheap, drab paint buckled and split. His sister hissed at him, then laughed, then probed her tongue around the inside of her mouth, as if trying to dislodge something crawling around in there. Now that their faces were separated by only two inches of tempered glass, Chuck could clearly see the scratches marring Ruth's once flawless skin, the clumps of blonde hair she'd torn from her once buoyant bouffant.

"Ruthie?" Chuck said lamely.

Ruth backed away from the door and said, "Did ya hear the one about the spiders?"

Chuck absentmindedly shook his head no and watched his sister disappear into the crushing black shadows of her padded cell.

"They're under my skin, Chuck-O."

And that was the moment Chuck knew he'd never laugh again. He tore his eyes away from the space where his sister had vanished and ran down the remaining length of the insane asylum. Fists pounded and throats hollered behind the series of doors as Chuck fled past them. It was as if the poor lost souls—lost souls like his sister's—could somehow pick up on Chuck's current emotional state. It was as if they'd been deprived of their gruel for weeks and now fed on his sickly sweet terror.

Chuck forced himself to slow down. He walked cautiously forward to where he thought the exit to this ward might be located. The frenzy around him lessened somewhat, but some of the afflicted inhabitants of those cells still howled in protest.

"I don't want my drum," said one of the patients, who was clearly in his late sixties. "I promise to be good. I want my mommy back."

"DA-FAAAAAAY-GO!" shouted another. "DA-FAAAAAAAAY-GO!"

Toward the end of the corridor, Chuck encountered an older assortment of cells. These ones had no doors or windows but instead featured corroded metal bars akin to those found in an abandoned prison. Within one such confinement, a man tracked Chuck's movements with a dead stare. A hollow smile then appeared instantaneously on his face, in total contrast to the rest of the man's dour affect.

Chuck's eyes drifted to the other side of the hall, where another deeply disturbed individual yanked off patches of his own scalp, stopping only long enough to look at the boy on the other side of the bars, whose face had drained of all color. Chuck could tell from the patchwork of scars on the man's skull that this tonsorial mutilation was a daily ritual.

Two warm globs then flew from opposite sides of the hall, synchronized to strike Chuck at the same moment. The smell hit Chuck well before he looked down and saw the brown smears on his stolen white doctor's coat.

"That's fine. I deserved that," Chuck said, remembering what he'd done to Tommy Milner on Halloween.

He backed up before more human feces could be sent his way, only to see the battle-ax nurse from the reception desk, followed by another squad of orderlies. Her orthopedic shoes squeaked against the ammonia-soaked floors. She pointed at Chuck and said, "I knew it. Grab him. And there are two more."

Chuck bolted down the remaining stretch of the psych ward. Arms—some scarred, some riddled with poxy blisters—shot out from behind the bars and snatched at Chuck. If he had been in a joking mood, Chuck might've made some comment like, "Uh, when she said, 'Grab him' I think she was talking to the staff—not the patients."

But Chuck felt as humorless as he did trapped, so he kept mum. The sordid hands got ahold of his doctor's coat, but Chuck tore it off and kept running. He hooked a sharp turn and barged through a door labeled "Staircase." As the nurse, orderlies, and treatment subjects of Pennhurst all shrieked after him, Chuck charged onto the pitch-black spiral of stairs.

He fumbled his way up a few flights (he lost count in his panic) and eventually exited onto another of the hospital's apparently endless supply of long corridors. But at least this one was empty. Chuck paused a moment to catch his breath, nearly hyperventilating from the exertion and the memory of what had become of Ruth.

As he doubled over, chest heaving, body hot and sweating under his clothing, Chuck failed to notice the subtle changes to his environment. Shadows that shouldn't have existed at nighttime crept into the corridor, sliding across the ceilings, walls, and floors, as if cast by another array of prison bars.

And the body heat wafting off Chuck traveled in waves up to the ceiling, which started to melt. White paint and plaster slowly dripped from its surface. The liquid beads fattened and gathered into trickling rivulets. And those rivulets took on the aspects of the heels and toes belonging to two padded feet. Those feet then pushed out of the ceiling, followed by legs.

Behind Chuck's back, a humanoid shape slid down

the wall to the floor. It was like some full-grown
monstrosity birthed by the hospital itself.

Alarms then went off across all of Pennhurst,
making Chuck jump. It wasn't just how loud the klaxons
were, although their blare was earsplitting. No, it was
how the alarms' corresponding lights caused everything—the walls, floors, doors, ceilings, even Chuck
himself—to turn red. He cried out in revulsion and
stormed away just before the shape could touch him.

"Help!" Chuck yelled. "*Help!* HELP!"

He hoped he might see Stella and Ramón barrel
out of one of the doors with the key to sparing all
of their lives. Hell, Chuck would've even settled for
the battle-ax nurse and her thuggish orderlies. But
no one came for Chuck.

Except the pale lady.

She stood at the distant end of the hallway
before him, the paint and plaster solidifying into
the body from his nightmares. Black, unkempt hair
spilled down her head and framed her equally
black eyes, which were set too far apart to be
human. She grinned mirthlessly at Chuck, and her
round belly shook with muted laughter, swaying her
diaphanous gown.

The pale lady took a step toward Chuck, and he
spun around to run the other way.

Only, the pale lady now waited for him at the
opposite end of the hall.

Chuck turned his head back and forth, looking
both ways. The pale lady somehow staggered toward
him from each direction at once. It was like there
were two of her, only, Chuck felt deep in his soul
that there was only one. But no matter where he
looked, the pale lady stood before him, getting
closer with each glance.

Noticing a third hallway branching off from the
main two, he flailed down it. But there she was again.

The pale lady.

Chuck scrambled backward, tried opening all of the locked doors around him.

"Help! *Help!* HELP!" he shouted again.

Chuck knew he was awake. Yet Chuck knew this was his dream too.

His head spun. But wherever Chuck looked, she looked back at him with her black eyes and inscrutable grin. He felt all of Pennhurst Hospital closing in on him—the deepening shadows, the incessant alarms, the red room, the pale lady stepping nearer, ever nearer.

It doesn't make any sense, Chuck thought.

She shuffled toward Chuck, only feet away. Then inches. The pale lady opened her arms as if to greet Chuck in an embrace. And then Chuck remembered.

Jokes don't have to make any sense.

Chuck backed against a wall, nowhere left to run, no place left to hide. The pale lady wrapped her gelatinous arms around him and enveloped his entire body into her own.

As long as they're funny.

"Did ya ever hear the one about my mom? She smothers me so much, I tell ya, I feel like one of her Salisbury steaks! Get it?"

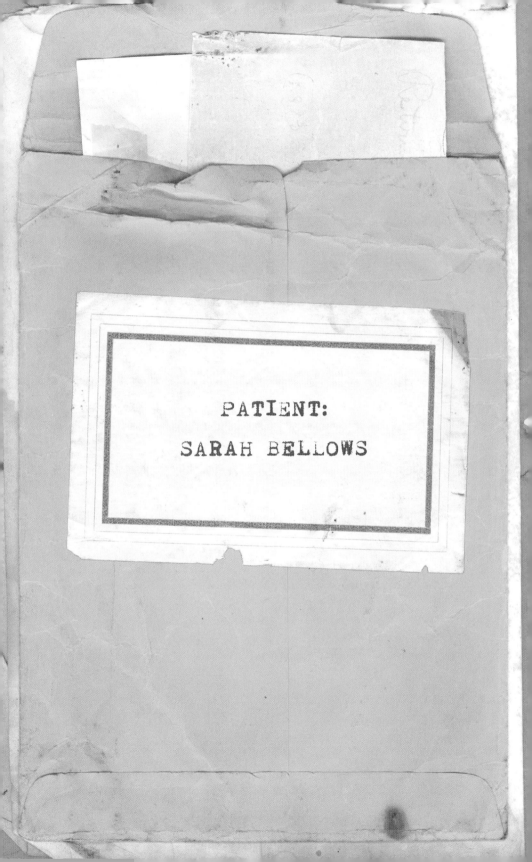

PATIENT:

SARAH BELLOWS

1

PENNHURST HOSPITAL

Whether transferred. *No*	Supervising Doctor. *Dr. Ephraim Bellows*

Name of Patient. *Sarah Bellows*	Age. *22*	Admitted. *December 8 1898*

Residence at or immediately previous to *Bellows House, Mill Valley*	Rank, Profession or Occupation. *no occupation*

Degree of Education *no formal*	Religious Persuasion. *Christian*	Married, Single or Widowed. *single*	Number of Children. *—*	Age of youngest Child. *—*

Whether the first Attack. *yes*	Age on first Attack *7*	Duration of existing Attack *2 months*	How many previous Attacks *several ongoing*

Confined in any Lunatic Asylum. *no*	Where	When	And how long

Supposed cause of Insanity. *Exhibits ongoing abnormal behavior*	Predisposing *Lack of basic impulse control* Exciting

Whether suicidal *undetermined*	Whether dangerous to others and in what way. *criminal predisposition to violence*

State of Bodily Health *indifferent*	Whether of sober habits *yes*	Relatives afflicted with Insanity. *no*

URGENCY CERTIFICATE (if any). *Dr. Ephraim Bellows, December 8*
   a. Facts indicating Insanity observed by myself at the time of Examination, viz.— *Patient displays signs of insanity, claiming to see spectral visions and displaying extreme mood swings. In my opinion, she appears to glow with a frenzied, fiend-like merriment.*
   b. Facts communicated by others. *Is guilty of committing homicidal acts against children, with no signs of remorse.*

1ST MEDICAL CERTIFICATE. *Dr. Ephraim Bellows, December 9.*
   a. Facts indicating Insanity observed by myself at the time of Examination, viz.— *I found her excited and restless with exaggerated ideas. Sleeps badly. Has exalted ideas. At times abuse and destructive. Clearly a danger to herself and others.*
   b. Facts communicated by others. *Recommend a routine of electroshock, isolation therapy, lateral cerebral diathermia treatment.*

2ND MEDICAL CERTIFICATE. *Dr. Ephraim Bellows.*
   a. Facts indicating Insanity observed by myself at the time of Examination, viz.— *as above*

   b. Facts communicated by others.

Discharged	Left	Died

2

PENNHURST HOSPITAL

Relation of Informant to Patient

FAMILY HISTORY

Insanity or other Diseases of Nervous System *Relatives have no history of mental defect.*

Phthisis

Alcoholism

Diabetes

Other Diseases

} *none*

PREVIOUS HISTORY

Neuroses in Patient *neuritis which began in early childhood*

Acute Rheumatism or Chorea

Fits—epileptic or hysterical *prone to hysteria*

„ infantile

Fevers *medication prescribed*

Syphilis *none* Catamenia *none*

Other Diseases *albinism*

Intemperate *yes*

Number and nature of previous attacks *exhibits ongoing abnormal behavior. exalted ideas. at times abusive and destructive*

Injuries or shocks *bruising, exacerbated by albinism*

Age and Sex of Children *none*

PRESENT ATTACK.

Time of earliest symptoms *originating in early childhood*

Nature of earliest symptoms *neuritis*

Progress of case *patient shows continuing signs of a predilection towards violence*

Suicidal or Dangerous (facts)

undetermined

ON ADMISSION.

Presence or absence of Bruises *Excessive bruising.*

Tongue *dry* Palate and Teeth *discolored*

Appetite *is unwilling to take food*

Bowels *inconsistent*

Abdominal Viscera *nothing abnormal detected*

Pelvic Viscera *no abnormalities.*

Catamenia

Urine *acid, 1010, no alb or sugar.*

Heart, Pulse, etc, *first sound impure at apex*

Lungs *normal*

Eyes and Sight

Pupils *contracted, equal, do not react to light*

Ears and Hearing

Taste and Smell

Common Sensation

Dynamometer

Handwriting

} *require further analysis*

Walk

Reflexes

Temperature *97* Speech *slow, voice low*

Weight *90 pounds.*

Sleep *infrequent* Dreams *abnormal, need further analysis*

Reaction to questions

Memory, Recent *problemed* Remote *yes*

Delusions, Exaltation *yes* Depression *yes*

Delusions relating to Digestion or food *requires further analysis*

Poison *no* Obstruction *no*

Hallucinations of Taste and Smell. *Refusal to eat indicates cognitive problems*

3

ELECTROSHOCK TREATMENT RECORD
PENNHURST HOSPITAL FOR THE INSANE

PATIENT NAME _Sarah Bellows_ PHYSICIAN _Dr. Ephraim Bellows_

Day	Time a.m.	Time p.m.	No. Shocks	Resistance	Voltage	Glissando Time	Duration of shock (seconds)	Type of Response	Grand Mals to date	Medication and Clinical Notes
Dec 9	7		1	—	120	1.6	.20	Gm++	1	a60 —
Dec 11		3	1		120	1.6	.15	Gm+	2	a70 —
Dec 13		2	1		120	1.6	.15	Gm	3	a70 —
Dec 15	9		1	—	120	1.6	.15	Gm	4	a70 —
Dec 18	8		1	—	120	1.6	.15	Gm	5	a70 —
Dec 21	10		1		120	1.6	.15	Gm	6	a70 —
Dec 23		12	1	—	120	1.6	.15	Gm	7	a70 —
Dec 25	8		1		120	1.6	.15	Gm	8	a60 —
Dec 27	11		1		120	1.6	.15	Gm+	9	a60 —
Dec 31		6	2	—	120/140	1.6	.15/.25	Gm++	10	a70 —
Jan 2		12	1	—	120	1.6	.15	Gm	11	a70 —
Jan 4	11		1	—	120	1.6	.15	Gm+	12	a60 —
Jan 6	10		1	—	120	1.6	.15	Gm	13	a70 —
Jan 8	8		1	—	120	1.6	.15	Gm	14	a70 —
Jan 10	8		1	—	120	16	.15	Gm	15	a60 —
Jan 12		12	1	—	120	1.6	.15	Gm	16	a70 —
Jan 14	8		1	—	120	1.6	.15	Gm	17	a70 —
Jan 16	8		1	—	120	16	.15	Gm	18	a60 —
Jan 20	11		1	—	120	1.6	.15	Gm+	19	a60 —
Jan 23	10		1	—	120	1.6	.15	Gm	20	a70 —

The Bellows Family on account of

Sarah Bellows

189

To Pennhurst Hospital, Dr.

				21
				31
To Pins & Elastics				
Cord, Elastics, & Tooth Brush			3.00	68 14
Dress support				68-66

Credit By Discount with state

34 07
$ 34 59

Mill Valley, December 8th 189 8

The Bellows Family

Dear Sirs; The balance due for the support

of Sarah Bellows at the Pennhurst Hospital for the

Insane is Thirty-four 54 Dollars, as per bill above
100

Yours Respectfully, Dr Ephraim Bellows

P. S. All Bills must be settled promptly. Drafts and Checks to be made payable to Pennhurst Hospital, and all remittances, (except the first payment,) and all Packages and Letters relating to clothing must be sent to our care.

8

Form 20-Med. Dec., 1886

PATIENT NOTES
PENNHURST HOSPITAL FOR THE INSANE

Name *Sarah Bellows*

Reg. No **156·076**
Date of Reception Order **Dec 8th**

Admitted	Cause.		Supervising Doctor
	Moral.	Physical	
December 8th	B.C.		Dr. Ephraim Bellows

Dec 9th — Electroshock Treatment
Patient came quietly to the examining room, seating herself voluntarily. She is very delusional and goes into a wealth of troubles regarding her family. Patient was given a series of electroshock treatments, followed by observation. Patient became despondant.

Dec 10th — Isolation Therapy
Patient pays little attention to questions asked. Her orientation was fairly intact as well as her memory for recent and remote events. She shows a degree of personal delapitation for it would seem that deterioration is gradually occurring. Patient was given 6 hours of isolation therapy.

Dec 11 — Lateral Cerebral Diathermia Treatment
Patient becoming less coherent in thinking and speech. Showing signs of depression and agitation. Denies all statements in the commitment papers. Explanations show signs of delusional thinking. Degrading condition calls for a treatment of lateral cerebral diathermia immediately. Patient remains despondant and shows no sign of improvement.

Office and Laboratory of

Dr. Ephraim Bellows,

Pennhurst Hospital

OFFICE HOURS:
8 to 10 A.M., 2 to 4 P.M.

Book _R_ Folio _1226_

Mill Valley. *December* 1898

Dearest Sir,

Your kind favour has been received. I believe that in the case of Sarah Bellows, the best remedy would be to pursue electro-shock therapy to cure Sarah of her insanity. Unfortunately her mind is far too plagued with anger, aggression, and is not following basic narratives and conversation.

It has been documented that electro-shock pulses to parts of the brain that produce those emotions can cure, or at least remedy the ill behavior of the mentally insane. Sarah Bellows is the perfect candidate for this treatment, because without it she is a danger to the civilians of Mill Valley.

101

Ward Admission Record

PENNHURST HOSPITAL FOR THE INSANE

Form 24-Med. Oct., 1886

Name *Sarah Bellows* Receiving Nurse *J. Gillespie* Ward **237**

Admitted *December 8* 19 **98** , at **1 P** M. Bathed at *1-30* PM.

TENDENCIES: **Homicidal** Violent Suicidal Depressed

CONDITION OF PERSON: (General nutrition, Cleanliness, Vermin, etc.)

Physical condition good.
Mites in hair. *(Achromasia Albinism)*

SKIN: (Marks, Bruises, Scars, Skin Diseases, Eruption and Locality)

Slight discoloration on extremities
Rash on left arm, scratching

PHYSICAL DISORDERS: (Deformities, Ruptures, Fractures, Dislocations, etc.)

Quality and Condition of clothing

Overall fair

Articles found on person

none

RETURN THIS SHEET TO OFFICE

Weight **57**
Height **5 ¼**
Temp. **99**
Pulse **104**
Resp. **26**

(Signed) *Jean Gillespie* NURSE

Name
Age
Diet
Case Bo

Char
Decen

Date of admissi
December
Result

102

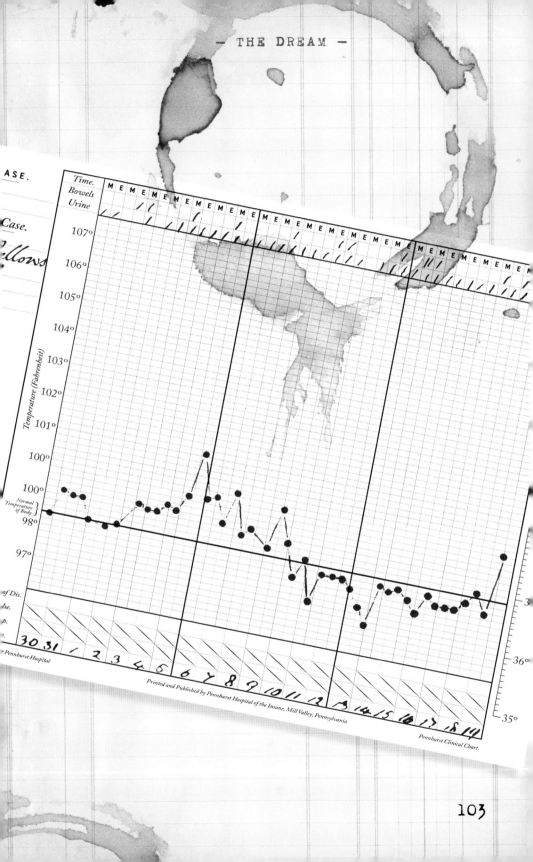

PENNHURST HOSPITAL
ASYLUM FOR THE INSANE

MILL VALLEY, PENNSYLVANIA

In the Matter of the Examination and Commitment of

Sarah Bellows

an Insane Person.

} COMPLAINT.

To the Dr. *Ephraim Bellows*, Doctor of said Facility:

The undersigned petitioner respectfully represents and shows to you that *I am* householder of this state; that *said* *Sarah Bellows* is an *insane* person, and by reason of *such insanity* *is unsafe to be at large.*

and is a proper subject for confinement in the Insane Asylum of this State

Pennsylvania

Wherefore, Your petitioner prays that you cause said *Sarah* *Bellows* to be brought before you, at such place as you may direct, and due inquiry made as prescribed by the matters alleged in this petition.

STATE OF PENNSYLVANIA } 89.
COUNTY OF MILL VALLEY

The petitioner above named, being first duly sworn, say that the foregoing petition is true *I* verily believe.

Deodat Bellows

{D.-1}

104

4

PENNHURST HOSPITAL — PATIENT MENU

DAY	BREAKFAST	DINNER	TEA
Dec 9	Sausages fried, Oatmeal, Tea	Pea soup Roast Beef Rice Pudding	Cold beef Tea
Dec 10	Irish stew Oatmeal Coffee	Roast Mutton Mince-meat Plum pudding.	Sweet Scones Tea
Dec 11	Sausages curried Oatmeal Coffee	Steak and kidney pie Vegetables Rice pudding	Corned beef Tea
Dec 12	Stewed steak & Bacon Oatmeal Tea	Vegetable soups Roast beef Bread Pudding	Cheese Tea
Dec 13	Loin chops fried Oatmeal Tea	Baked rabbit Mince-meat Tapioca custard	Brawn Tea
Dec 14	Brazed mutton Oatmeal Coffee	Cold corned beef Vegetables Rice custard	Tea-cakes Tea
Dec 15	Sausages fried Oatmeal Tea	Vegetable soup Roast Mutton Bread Pudding	Cold potato pie Tea
Dec 16	Stewed Mutton Oatmeal Coffee	Steak & Kidney pie Vegetables. Fruit Pie	Sweet scones. Tea
Dec 17	Fried rump Steak Oatmeal Tea	Pea soup Roast beef Baked rice custard	Cheese Tea
Dec 18	Irish Stew Oatmeal Tea	Boiled fish Vegetables Macaroni Custard	Brawn Tea
Dec 19	Curried mutton Oatmeal Coffee	Baked rabbit Mince-meat Prunes	Sweet Scones + Tea

PENNHURST HOSPITAL

PATIENT: Bellows, S.

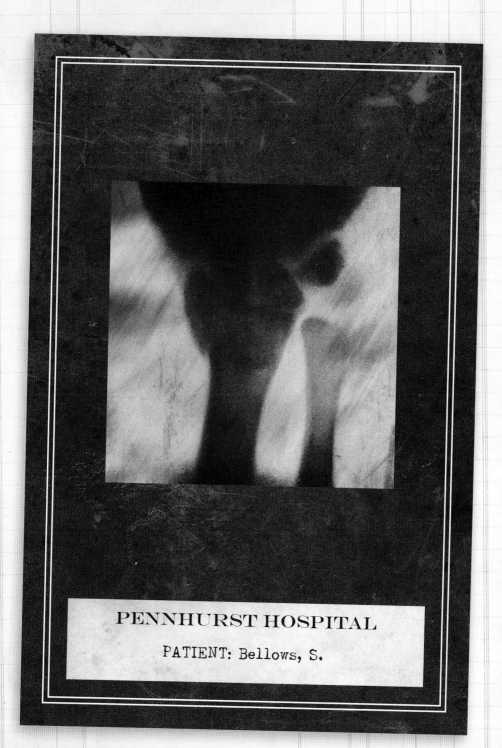

PENNHURST HOSPITAL

PATIENT: Bellows, S.

PENNHURST HOSPITAL

PATIENT: Bellows, S.

PENNHURST HOSPITAL

PATIENT: Bellows, S.

SARAH AS SHE LOOKED WHEN SHE READ TO THE
CHILDREN AND WROTE STORIES

SARAH WAS ABLE TO
STAND AND WALK
BUT IT WAS VERY
PAINFUL —

SO SHE WAS IN
A CUSTOM WHEEL
CHAIR —

INK STAINS —
HANDS/CLOTHES

VINCENT PROCE

RAH IN LIFE –

HAIR COVER GROWTH

SHOCK OF WHIT
HAIR GROWS
OUT OF
GROW

RACE KEEPSHER
EAD AND SPINE
STRAIGHT

STAINS

VINCENT PROCE

Me Tie Dough-ty Walker

w

he

io

mid

off

this:

"M

"It

but

it sa

"W

Turn

had never

later, he heard

and louder, but

"Me tie dough

This time the ma

answering. He was afr

would hear it and com

But his dog paid no

"Wee rai sowly raw

Ramón Morales always assumed he'd die young. And when he finally turned eighteen, that suspicion cemented into fact.

Driving his 1963 Rambler Ambassador had been Ramón's one escape from the certainty he faced. Yet even on those empty lanes, those bucolic back roads, he had no trouble in imagining his own death. Usually, the scenarios involved the explosion of a hidden land mine, like the ones waiting for him overseas. Or he might envision being pummeled unconscious by the bloody hands of some arrogant, entitled bigot, like that Tommy Milner kid.

But no matter how far he drove or how fast he pushed the engine, Ramón never once expected that his death would be foretold in the pages of an old book.

Then again, he probably wouldn't change a thing about his life, drastically shortened though it might be. Because in finding that cursed book, Ramón also found the one person who treated Ramón like he, too, was a person. Not just a Social Security number on a draft letter or a teen with dark skin who fit some preconceived profile of how a criminal should appear.

No, when Stella looked at Ramón, she made him feel like he had a future. A life. For as long as it would last, anyway...

Ramón rested his head on the holding cell bars. He felt the metal vibrate against his skull as another peal of thunder rumbled outside. Rain pelted against the police station's roof and windows, making the cinderblock walls seem all the grayer. The only warmth in the place came from the fireplace in the corner. And from Stella, who occupied the cell next to Ramón's.

With nothing else left to do but await the inevitable, Ramón's mind drifted back to when he first

arrived in Mill Valley four nights ago. He'd been
driving due north ever since he received his draft
papers in the mail.

It wasn't just that Ramón was afraid to die. He
was. He had seen enough friends return from combat
in pieces, in body bags. But no, what scared Ramón
more than losing his own life was taking the life of
another. Yes, he was scared of dying. But he was even
more scared of killing.

Ramón had witnessed enough bloodshed in his
hometown to last multiple lifetimes. He'd seen guys
get stabbed in knife fights with other gangs. He'd
studied the scars left by those gashes and the terri-
ble stitchwork done by incompetent doctors the poor
could barely afford. He'd watched cousins suffer
"misunderstandings" with the police, then get carted
off to serve time for crimes they did not commit.

And now Ramón was expected to do what, exactly?
Fly off to the other side of the world and rob
other families of their sons? He struggled to recon-
cile those impersonal, neatly typed marching orders.
How could he defend his country on foreign soil
when his country couldn't defend people like him in
their own neighborhoods?

The trek to Canada had taken Ramón up through
the entire length of Florida, and the path made him
think of a funny saying he'd heard back in his old
stomping grounds.

"In Florida, the farther north you go, the deeper
south you get."

The sight of Confederate flags still billowing
in front of courthouses made Ramón want to push
the pedal to the metal. Yet he didn't want to go so
fast that he'd get pulled over, either. Those good ol'
boy sheriffs Ramón passed in each town didn't look
like the patient or understanding sort. That's why
he obeyed every speed limit, signaled each turn,
and kept his eyes on the road, stopping only long

enough to refuel, and only when it was absolutely necessary, at that.

The pattern continued through Georgia, the Carolinas, and beyond. Ramón dared not rest until he got as far north as his bleary eyes would allow. Reaching Mill Valley, Pennsylvania, he decided that the sleepy little town was as safe a place as any above the Mason-Dixon Line to stop. Except Ramón didn't like the way Chief Turner eyed him when the Rambler turned down Main Street. The lawman's glare reminded him a little too much of the incriminating looks he received in the Southern states.

Ramón figured his best bet was to park at the drive-in, pretend to take in a couple of Halloween movies while he slept, and then be back on the road before the sun came up. He must've only been out for a few minutes when Stella and her friends hopped into Ramón's car. The sight of the girl dressed as a witch—and the fear in her eyes—jolted Ramón awake faster than any *cafecito.*

Stella and two boys had been on the run from a local bully. Ramón knew the type. He'd had to fight off a few himself back in the day, only to take the blame for the bully's aggression each and every time. So, when Tommy Milner caught up with Stella and the others and started banging on the Rambler's windshield, Ramón wanted to deck him immediately.

But Ramón knew that he shouldn't. That he couldn't. Because even though it was Tommy who was instigating violence, Ramón would be the one found at fault by a jury not comprised of his peers. Ramón didn't want that just as much as he didn't want to be zipped into an army body bag. Not now. Not this close to Canada.

No, Ramón decided to keep his cool. Keep his head down. Keep his eyes on the road.

He drove Stella, Chuck, and Auggie to the one
place they thought they'd be left alone—some crumbling old mansion they called the Bellows house. It
was there that Stella found the book, just as she'd
found Ramón. It was there that the stories within its
arcane pages began to claim the lives of those who'd
wandered into the Bellows estate.

If the book didn't get him, some bloodthirsty
Mill Valley mob would. Now that people were disappearing, Chief Turner had locked up Ramón and
Stella and was already building his case. Hispanic
kid blows into town, a switchblade in his possession,
local kids go missing—open-and-shut, really. And the
chief's exhibit A would be the Bellows book, which
he pored through at the front of the station. Ramón
could hear Turner scoffing from his cell.

"Me Tie Dough-Ty Walker?" he heard the chief ask
aloud in confusion.

Lightning flashed outside, and more thunder
rattled the holding cell bars. Ramón and Stella
exchanged an apprehensive look. They then heard
Chief Turner's imperious footsteps approach the
holding area, followed by the trotting gait of his
dog, Trigger.

Of course he named his dog Trigger, Ramón
thought in resignation.

"Which one of you comes up with sick stuff like
this?" Turner asked while brandishing the book he'd
confiscated from them. "Is it you, Stella?"

The chief had asked her the question, but his
eyes remained bored into Ramón's. It didn't matter
how Stella answered Turner's question. There was no
way the policeman was going to let a draft dodger
slip through his fingers. Let alone one with a name
like Ramón Morales.

"We didn't write them," Stella said.

But no sooner had she spoken than the station's
lights flickered out, drowning the holding cells

121

in darkness, save for the fireplace. More lightning flashed outside, trailed in quick succession by
a booming thunderclap and even heavier rainfall.
Ramón guessed that Chief Turner would attribute the
power outage to the storm, not the book in his hands.

Trigger, on the other hand, seemed far less trou-
bled by the dark. The dog curled up in front of the
fireplace. A log splintered in the heat, issuing a
cascade of embers that trailed up the hearth's chimney. Silence followed, yet Trigger suddenly sat ram-
rod straight and stared at the fireplace. He cocked
his head and raised an ear. It seemed he was expecting something.

Chief Turner looked like he was about to call
Trigger to his side, when the dog started to make a
noise. But he wasn't trying to growl.

He was trying to talk.

"Wee rai rowly rawer," said Trigger the dog.

Normally, the sound of a talking dog would've
sent Ramón into hysterics. But that was before he
entered Mill Valley. That was before he encountered
the book that worked its witchcraft upon those
unfortunate enough to read it.

Chief Turner didn't seem too amused either, saying, "How'd you make him do that?"

He cast another accusatory glare at Ramón, who
locked eyes with Stella in turn. Once again, they
said more to each other with a look than most people
conveyed with words, even though the two teens had
only met a few days ago.

"What's the story?" Ramón asked the chief. "What
happens in the story?"

Chief Turner considered the new chapter that he'd
been reading, the one that he hadn't noticed when he
first gained possession of the book. The one with
the nonsense title.

"LYNCHEE-KINCHY, COLLY-MOLLY, DINGO-DINGO!"
Trigger said before whimpering at the fireplace.

"What in Jesus's name is going on?" Chief Turner
wailed.

"WEE RAI ROWLY RAWER!" answered Trigger, eyeing
the hearth in alarm. "LYNCHEE-KINCHY, COLLY-MOLLY,
DINGO-DINGO!"

"What happens in the story? Whose name is in the
book?" Stella demanded from her cell.

The chief, spooked into a stunned stupor, looked
down at the book. But Ramón knew what he was going
to say before Turner even read it. Ramón knew it
was his name written in Sarah Bellows's book.

Trigger stopped talking and recoiled from the
fireplace just as a thumping noise echoed down the
chimney. Something heavy and horribly hollow-sound-
ing rolled out of the flue, kicking up ash and coming to a stop on the floor outside the holding cells.

It was a head.

"Are you shitting me?" Chief Turner moaned.

The head, with its quilt of mismatched flesh
patches and wisps of straggly gray hair, split into
a toothsome grin and said, "Me Tie Dough-Ty Walker!"

Turner dropped the book and fumbled for his ser-
vice pistol, then took aim at the leering disembodied
skull. The chief of police then emptied his firearm
into the head, shooting holes through it, until the
chamber clicked. The bullets had been spent, but
still the head said, "Me Tie Dough-Ty Walker!"

Its cataract eyes looked back to the fireplace, where a pair of decomposing feet spilled out of the hearth, followed by legs of differing lengths and skin tones. Clearly, they had originated from two separate bodies. Ramón then imagined a platoon of soldiers ascending ropes to the police station's roof, unzipping black body bags slung over their backs, and dumping the contents down the chimney.

"Let us out!" Stella implored.

But Chief Turner remained rooted in place, watching as those legs toppled forward more times than they should have. They attached themselves to the stumps on the feet.

More random parts rained down with fleshy thuds—a torso, arms, and hands. They all wriggled forward and assembled under the head. Gangrenous skin and sinew wove together in a depraved mockery of the healing process. The bent figure of a man finally stood of its own volition, the gibbering head worn upside down.

"ME TIE DOUGH-TY WALKER!" the Jangly Man shouted again.

It spasmed toward the paralyzed Chief Turner and raised him bodily off the ground. The policeman had enough time to scream in fright before the Jangly Man snapped his neck. The simulacrum then threw Chief Turner's limp body against Stella's bars. Turner landed in an unceremonious heap on the cold station floor, much in the way his killer had done so only moments ago.

Ramón and Stella exchanged one last look of dread from across their respective cells. They then watched as the lopsided head regarded them from below. The Jangly Man crab-walked on all fours across the jail, sniffing the air as its fingers and toes undulated in millipede coordination.

The obscene thing briefly paused to notice Stella before moving on to the next cage. Ramón backed against the corner of his cell as the Jangly Man left the floor and began crawling up the bars. While Stella reached out toward Chief Turner's inert body, Ramón grabbed the one piece of furniture not bolted to the ground—a stool—and wielded it like the poorest excuse for a weapon ever.

Clinging upside down to the cell, the Jangly Man began forcing his asymmetrical face through the iron bars. Ramón thought he could hear the crunch of bones before the impossible being once again said, "ME TIE DOUGH-TY WALKER!"

"Jesus Christ," Ramón muttered while standing clear.

He vaguely perceived Stella shouting at him and him shouting something back across their cells. But Ramón's eyes remained glued to the Jangly Man, who had shoved his skull past the bars, followed by a dislocated shoulder. Next, ribs snapped this way and that as the chest cavity compressed and squeezed into Ramon's cell.

"COWARD!" the Jangly Man screeched with a swipe of his arm.

Ramón dodged the jagged, groping fingernails, then spotted Stella again. Only, she was outside of her own cell now, desperately trying to open Ramón's with the late chief's keys.

The Jangly Man had pulled most of himself through the bars. All that remained was a protruding hip and the accompanying leg, which leaked pus everywhere. Ramón grimaced, feeling the abomination's graveyard breath on his face, then looked back at Stella.

She fit the right key into the lock, turned it, and flung open the cell door. It slammed against the adjacent bars with a resounding clang, momentarily disorienting the Jangly Man. Ramón chucked the stool, ducked another fitful grab from those rotted hands, and scrambled out of the cell.

Stella reclaimed the Bellows book off the floor where it had been dropped, while Ramón reclaimed his switchblade—and Chief Turner's car keys. They ran past the booking desk and out of the station, with the writhing Jangly Man left trapped between

the bars—until its body spontaneously disassem-
bled. The various components dropped to the ground
inside and outside of Ramón's former cell, then
started worming toward each other again.

Ramón and Stella burst through the station's front
doors. Rain fell in droves, soaking them. Yet the book
in Stella's arms remained strangely bone-dry.

"Hurry!" Stella yelled as they rushed toward
Turner's police cruiser.

Ramón stopped just shy of unlocking the doors.
He wanted to protect Stella just as he had on
Halloween night. Just as she had protected Ramón
in the holding cell and every other waking moment
he spent in Mill Valley. But Ramón realized that his
fate had already been written. He'd known it before
some army secretary licked the envelope that held
his draft letter. If he let Stella stay with him, he'd
only be putting her in danger.

This was one more ride Ramón would have to
take alone.

"What're you waiting for?" Stella asked.

"Go to her house," Ramón said.

He didn't even need to say the name. The words "Sarah Bellows" transmitted wordlessly between them, as so many other things had in the span of four short nights.

"Tell her the truth," Ramón said to Stella. "That thing will follow me."

Stella checked nervously over her shoulder, but the police station remained eerily still. As much as it pained her to admit it, she said, "The stories come true every time."

"Then you better run fast," Ramón replied, more to save Stella than to save himself. "Stop her and you will stop this."

More silent understanding passed across the space separating them. Ramón watched Stella push aside her conflicted feelings and run away from him, toward the storm. He then climbed behind the cruiser's steering wheel, twisted the key in the ignition, and heard the engine turn over.

Fighting every survival instinct he possessed, Ramón waited, waited, waited ... until the Jangly Man sprawled out of the station. It roared its inhuman cry, followed by the clash of another bolt of lightning.

Ramón slammed the car into drive and floored the gas. The cruiser fishtailed on the wet asphalt and sped away, with the Jangly Man galloping after in frantic pursuit.

It felt good to break the speed limit for a change. If Ramón was going down on this night, he was going down swinging. He pushed every button and switch he could see on the dashboard, stopping only once he'd activated the rooftop siren. Red and blue lights pulsed around the rain-streaked surroundings, giving Ramón a strobe-like view of the dark road around him. He then heard a faint whine come from behind.

Ramón looked through the patrol car's rearview mirror and saw Trigger staring plaintively from the backseat. Rain matted the dog's fur, and Ramón angled the mirror to see one of the rear windows had been left rolled open earlier in the day.

"*Ay, que bueno,*" Ramón said sarcastically. "Listen, dog, if you start talking again, I'm driving us both straight to Pennhurst."

Trigger lowered his head in shame, and Ramón sighed. He pumped the brakes, and four tires skidded on the slicked road. Shaking his head, hardly believing what he was about to do, Ramón hopped out of the car. He opened the rear door from the outside, and Trigger leapt out of the back seat most gratefully.

"Go on, boy, go!" Ramón hollered as Trigger scampered into the nearby woods. "I hope your next owner isn't such an asshole!"

Ramón got back in the driver's seat, shifted into gear, and stomped hard on the gas pedal. Pistons pumped and fuel combusted under the hood, giving off so much horsepower, Ramón could feel it vibrating through the chassis. He topped sixty within seconds, then eighty, the red and blue lights still swirling as the cruiser tore through Mill Valley.

Even with the windshield wipers flicking back and forth at their fastest setting, Ramón had trouble seeing the road through the downpour. He squinted through the beaded glass, then felt the entire vehicle shudder with a loud bang. Ramón wondered if he'd flooded the engine and caused it to backfire.

His eyes saw a face in the windshield, and it was not his own reflection. The Jangly Man leered back from the outside of the cruiser. Its head had finally gone right side up and was close enough for Ramón to make out more of the details afflicting its appearance.

The two eyes bulged milky white around the pin-pricks that passed as their pupils. The wide mouth held so many teeth, it almost looked as if two different sets of jaws had been fused together. And a long, circuitous scar ran like a ragged seam down its face. Not even the most inexperienced field medic on any battlefield—or the most incompetent emergency room doctor in any ghetto—could have done a worse job patching a body back together.

The Jangly Man reached around and tried to open the driver's side door from the outside. But Ramón quickly pushed down on the door lock pin with his elbow, never letting up on the accelerator. Undeterred, the Jangly Man then punched and kicked in the windows. Glass and rain struck Ramón, and only now did he jam the brakes. The inertia sent the Jangly Man slipping down the cruiser and dangling across its front bumper.

Ramón watched the wretch's disparate parts all work in concert. Limbs from men and women tried to stabilize their gestalt form on the wet hood. Muscles flexed under an undead fabric that had been knitted together by skin both light and dark. In its

discordant motions, the Jangly Man represented to
Ramón everything that could be great about human-
ity—and all that was not.

The two figures stared at each other through the
windshield for a tense moment before Ramón put the
cruiser in drive yet again. Pulling hard to the side,
Ramón veered off the main road and struggled to
latch his seatbelt in time. The buckle clicked into
place just in time, and Ramón braced himself against
the steering wheel.

The Jangly Man had just enough time to swivel its
head around 180 degrees and see the parked semitruck.

Chief Turner's cruiser slammed into the side
of the truck, making an accordion of the cruiser's front end and blowing out all the windows and
tires. Ramón felt his body lurch forward, then get
sent back just as violently. But the safety belt
held, and he maintained consciousness. Slumping out
of the dented driver's side door in a daze, Ramón
got to his feet and looked back.

The Jangly Man was pinned between the ruined
cruiser and the semi. The uneven arms remained
motionless, and its misshapen head lolled to the
side. A moment later, the ramshackle body parts
self-amputated and fell. They landed lifelessly
in an iridescent puddle that was equal parts rain
water and gasoline.

Ramón Morales always assumed he'd die young.
And there was a good chance he still might. But in
the meantime, he would try to find Stella again. He
would do everything in his power to feel alive in
her presence for as long as possible. Ramón would
outrace death until he couldn't anymore.

He limped away from the crash and toward the
Bellows estate, on the run again.

The rain never let up. The severed body parts
tensed alive once more. And the Jangly Man dragged
after the boy who was no longer afraid to kill.

The Haunted House

The Haunted House

One time Stella went to see if she could put a haunt
to rest at a house in her settlement. The house had been
haunted for about ten years. Several people had tried to stay
there all night, but they always would get scared out by the
haunt.

So Stella took her Bible and went to the house —
went on in, built herself a good fire, and lit a lamp. Set
the _____ with Bible. The _____ before _____ heard

Stella Nicholls had written and read enough scary stories to know how most felt about haunted houses. Characters tended to run screaming from them, narrowly escaping with their lives—if not their sanity. But Stella had to be the one person to run *into* a haunted house, didn't she?

"Why are you doing this ... ?" she asked.

Although Stella couldn't be sure if that was meant for someone else ... or for herself. Stella thought she knew the answer, of course. She was chasing a ghost. Stella was always chasing a ghost, it seemed. Ever since she was a little girl. Ever since she was six.

And now, ten years later, here Stella stood, wet and shivering at the threshold of the Bellows estate. Wiping raindrops from her glasses and tightening her grip on the book in her hands, she treaded into the old mansion. Stella's shoes, still soaked from the storm, mingled with a veneer of dust on the creaking floorboards, leaving little muddy footprints behind her. She hoped she might be able to follow them back outside once she was done, like some breadcrumb trail from a fable. Provided Stella survived the night.

She felt those odds of survival drop considerably as she crept farther and farther inside the decaying home. Stella's dread stemmed in part from her surroundings. The few cobwebbed fixtures that hadn't been pilfered by looters over the years served as stark reminders of the family that once resided in these halls. With a steadying breath, Stella walked past a crooked, weathered portrait of the Bellows family. The painting captured the dour, miserable countenances of a father and mother, their two sons, and a grandmother. And one other figure stood apart from the rest, her hair and flesh

far whiter than theirs—a daughter, whose face and
body had been painted over by some frenzied hand.

    Sarah Bellows, thought Stella.

    Just thinking the name sent a new shudder
throughout Stella's waterlogged body. Gooseflesh
prickled down her arms, all the way to her finger-
tips. Stella was reminded of the weighty book still
clutched in her hands. Sarah's book.

    Stella had first encountered the tome a few
nights ago—Halloween night, to be exact—when she
and her friends had been on the run from Tommy
Milner. They'd barely avoided the bully at the Gorge
drive-in theater and were looking for a remote,
uninhabited spot to wait until Tommy's drunken ire
had faded—or until he passed out from one too many
beers, whichever came first. And Stella couldn't
think of any spot in Mill Valley more remote or
uninhabited than the old Bellows place.

    Everyone in town had heard the legends about
that house and the pale, reclusive witch who had
lived there. But Stella always harbored a special
affinity for the local lore and prided herself
on becoming something of an expert on all things
Bellows. Maybe it was because Sarah Bellows, apart
from being a witch who murdered the nearby children, was rumored to be an aspiring writer, just
like Stella. Or maybe it was because Stella's mom,
Dinah, was the one who always told her those scary
stories in the dark. Those ghastly bedtime tales
became something of a ritual for the two Nicholls
women and represented one of the few memories
young Stella still retained of her mother.

    But on this past Halloween, Tommy had managed to
track Stella's little band of misfits to the Bellows
estate and locked them in its cellar. Down there,
Stella and her reticent new acquaintance, Ramón, had
discovered the late Sarah Bellows's book. At first,
Stella had been thrilled to learn that she and Sarah

were, indeed, both young authors after all. Yet that
thrill quickly curdled into fear when new stories began appearing on the recovered tome's blank
pages—stories written with bloodred ink in Sarah's
phantom hand. Worse still, the grisly endings foretold in those added chapters began befalling Stella's
friends. Fiction became fact, and Stella soon realized that the local lore was more than just myths
grown-ups told to frighten their children into com-
pliance. These scary stories were real.

That realization prompted Stella's second trip to
the Bellows estate, the day after Halloween, when
she returned Sarah's book to the cellar. But no matter how many ways Stella tried to rid herself of
the accursed volume—losing it, burying it, burning
it—Sarah Bellows's book always came back unbidden
to Stella.

Turning a corner past the blighted family portrait, Stella saw the very same book still held in
her dripping, goose-pimpled hands. This return to the
Bellows manor marked Stella's third trip. She had
already tempted fate enough by coming here twice.
And with this final visit, she sensed her already slim
survival odds dropping the rest of the way down to
none. Yet as much as she wanted to, Stella couldn't
turn back now. If there was any chance to save herself, save Ramón, and potentially undo what had been
done to her best friends, Stella would have to keep
chasing that ghost just a little longer.

She pressed on, sidestepping a puddle on the
warped wood floor. Rain poured through the holes in
the wrecked roof and down past the rafters. The plaster had long since gone black with mold, and bent,
rusted nails wormed their way out of the bloated
baseboards. The house itself seemed to be a dying
thing to Stella, an ancient organism that was about to
breathe its last, then bury her under the weight of
its collapsed skeleton.

Stella forced the thought from her mind. Such an
overactive imagination came in handy while writing
her short stories, but Stella knew she needed her
head clear for whatever came next. Her senses on high
alert, Stella felt the wind howl through the mansion's
perforated walls like heavy sighs. She smelled mildew, tasted rot on the air, and heard more raindrops
patter onto the uneven floors.

But Stella's ears perked when that dripping became
a ticking, as if from some distant clock. That clock-
work ticking then became a faint, repetitive hiss, the
kind heard on old phonograph records. A song then
began to play, faded yet familiar. Unsettled by the
melody, Stella turned in place and watched the home
transform around her, as if revived by some fresh
jolt of life.

A warm glow washed over the house, restoring

luster to its architecture and decor. The foyer, once a cold and crumbling heap, renovated itself into a lavish entryway. The wainscoting and banisters gleamed with an oiled shine. And the wallpaper, formerly tattered and peeling, now lay flat on the walls, its gilded filigree reflecting the light from polished gas lamps. Stella was so stunned by the sight of the Bellows estate in its full glory, she scarcely noticed that Sarah's book had disappeared from her hands.

Dazed by the resplendent trappings, Stella wandered deeper. She touched the walls and the furniture as she went, all of it feeling vivid and incredibly real to her unencumbered fingers. The dripping, ticking, and hissing sounds were all gone now, replaced by the murmur of conversation. Stella padded closer to the burnished staircase and heard raised voices echoing above her.

"She's out of her room again," said a woman.

"Boys!" bellowed a man's voice in return. "Sarah's out!"

Stella's eyes flicked from the stairs to the Bellows family portrait hanging on the wall. It had been righted, and its oil paint glistened like new. Yet Sarah Bellows's face remained obliterated from the image. Hearing those quarreling voices above her head, Stella figured the woman's belonged to Sarah's severe mother, Delanie Bellows, while the man's belonged to Sarah's stone-faced father, Deodat Bellows.

Booming footsteps lumbered down the stairs, startling Stella. She backed away from the hall and into the household library. During Stella's initial foray on Halloween, the room had been a gutted cavern reeking of sodden newsprint and rife with silverfish. On this night, however, the space appeared like the

library of Stella's dreams. Its shelves held row after
row of leather-bound books. First edition printings
sat on display at the desk beside antique reading
lamps and magnifying glasses. Sarah even marveled at
the several plush tufted chairs nestled into the corners. She could almost imagine herself sitting in one
of them for hours on end—days, even—reading all of
the library's great works in alphabetical order. It
was only the approach of those thundering footsteps
that shook Stella from this reverie and reminded her
of the present circumstances.

Or *past circumstances,* Stella thought as she took
one last look at her surroundings from another time.

She ducked behind an ornate set of drapes just
before one of the brothers from the portrait,
the thickset one, barreled into the library. Even
through the fabric, Stella could hear him snapping
a leather strap in his hands with sadistic glee.

"I got your belt, Daddy!" the Bellows boy called
across the house.

Stella stifled a flinch when the belt snapped
again. She then heard the other brother barge in and
quarrel with his sibling. As they argued over who
would whip what part of Sarah's body and for how
long, Stella felt her stomach churn with an unset-
tling understanding. In all of the scary stories
her mom had told her as a child, Stella had always
known Sarah Bellows to be the villain, the ghoul,
the monster. But in hearing the Bellows brothers
describe in graphic detail how they intended to
torture their sister, Stella began to question the
bedtime tales that had so fueled her own writerly
ambitions. And even more immediately troubling, she
couldn't shake the feeling that the Bellows weren't
just talking about Sarah. It was almost as if they
were hunting for Stella as well.

The brothers set off anew in search of Sarah,
leaving Stella alone in the library once more. She
waited a moment, then slipped out from behind the
curtains and hurried back the way she came. Careful
not to telegraph her movements, Stella tiptoed
toward the estate entrance. She arrived at the foyer
just in time to see the Bellows family patriarch,
Deodat, lock the front door from the inside. As he
tucked the key into the taut vest hugging his belly,
Stella hesitated. She couldn't escape the house, nor
could she backtrack, as she heard Deodat's thuggish
sons circling around again. With no other options
left, Stella ascended lightly up the stairs before
Deodat Bellows's scrutinizing eye could spot her.

Reaching the second-story landing, Stella tried
the first door she could find. The knob turned easily, admitting her into a master bedroom. Stella
could barely see straight. Her vision throbbed in
rhythm with her beating heart, and all extremities
trembled with the surge of adrenaline coursing
through her system. If she could just get a moment
to think. To catch her breath. To—

"I hear her," rasped a dry, pitiless voice.

Stella spun around and saw the gaunt grandmother from the portrait. Gertrude Bellows sat in
her rocking chair opposite an elegant dresser, staring vacantly past the black lace veil that shrouded
her from head to toe. Stella's eyes bulged behind
her glasses, though she couldn't exactly blame herself for missing the crone on the way into the
room. It'd be difficult for anyone—even somebody
with twenty-twenty vision—to discern where the old
woman ended and the shadows around her began.

Sensing the intruder by the doorway, Gertrude
Bellows finally lifted her veil, revealing her own
eyes. Stella gasped. For both of the grandmother's
eyes were made of glass. The marbles looked dead
ahead, never swiveling in their sockets, never

blinking behind their wrinkled eyelids. Gertrude cocked her ear in Stella's direction and said, "You're writing those stories again, aren't you, you little brat!"

Despite her frail appearance, the elder Bellows rapped her cane upon the floor three times.

Thud.

Thud.

Thud.

"She's here!" cried Grandma Bellows. "She's in here!"

Stella was about to explain herself to the woman, to beg for some shred of understanding or leniency, when she caught her reflection in a wall mirror. Only, it wasn't Stella's face that stared back through the frame.

It was Sarah's.

Stunned speechless, Stella touched her face and watched a foreign, pale hand do the same thing in the mirror. Alabaster hair flowed over the reflection's face, obscuring most of Sarah's features. But not the cruel expression on her lips.

Stella's own mouth struggled to string together words, but none came. Instead, she fled the bedroom, shut the door behind her, and bolted around a corner. Standing behind an imposing grandfather clock, its ticking identical to the one Stella heard in her own era, she said a quick, silent prayer. Stella then strained to hear over the clock's inner workings, and eavesdropped on Deodat. The man had limped back upstairs upon hearing Gertrude's alarm and now bickered with her. It seemed to Stella that no one in the Bellows family shared a friendly word with any of their kin. At least Roy and Dinah Nicholls had always been civil with their daughter and with each other, all the way up to the night Stella's mom disappeared.

"Did you hear her?" Deodat demanded of his mother.

"She ran that way," Gertrude spat back.

Knowing she only had seconds to move—and that the hitch in Deodat's step would likely slow him down—Stella emerged from behind the clock. Clearly, there would be no reasoning with the Bellows under normal circumstances. And if Stella appeared to them the way she appeared in Gertrude's mirror—as the spitting image of their hated Sarah—then Stella doubted she'd be able to get a single word out before they wrapped their hands around her throat. That surety gave Stella the second wind needed to move her feet. She sped past the master bedroom, and rushed downstairs once more.

But the pitched voices of the other members of the Bellows clan greeted Stella as soon as she reached the first floor. They called out from all corners, alternately trying to coax Sarah from wherever she was hiding and threatening what they'd do once they found her. Their curses bounced off the coffered ceilings and marble balustrades, making Delanie and her sons sound like they were near Stella and coming ever closer.

The only location that seemed even remotely secure at the moment was the library. So, Stella stole back into the book-lined retreat, hoping that the Bellows boys hadn't returned with their strap and their murderous appetites. She dove beneath Deodat's desk, then heard his irregular footsteps pass down the hall, followed by those of his wife and offspring. Stella listened long enough to confirm they'd all moved on to another wing, then rose from under the desk. Her eyes scanned its surface, desperate to locate another key like Deodat's, but to no avail. All she saw were stacks of work documents—financial reports, elevation surveys, and telegrams from neighboring mills, all dated 1898. Stella rubbed her fingers on some of the forms and found the ink still wet.

It was all happening. For whatever reason, Stella was in Sarah's time. In Sarah's home. In Sarah's—

Wait, thought Stella, forcing her brain to calm and focus.

She saw a row of books on the desk. And even though they were newly bound with all of their crisp pages intact, Stella recognized them instantly. They were an exact match to Sarah Bellows's notebook of horrors. Stella could almost feel it in her hands anew. The one she'd found in the cellar had a cracked spine and brittle endpapers. But there was no mistaking it. Sarah's book made a complete set with those on her father's desk.

Overcome with curiosity, Stella took one of the volumes and flipped through it. Rather than being filled with more scary stories, its pages contained meticulous records of the Bellows' paper mill, the one that inspired Mill Valley's name so many years ago.

Or maybe Mill Valley hasn't even been named yet, Stella thought as she considered her current setting.

Her eyes narrowed as they scoured the rest of the business ledgers. The way Dinah always told it to Stella, Sarah Bellows's alleged sinister behavior had brought ruin to both her family name and business. Sarah's ultimate death had delivered some relief to the town, but not to its economy. The beleaguered Bellows mill shuttered not long after, and Mill Valley's fortunes had improved little in the decades since.

But in reviewing these notebooks in person, Stella saw a business flush with profit. Most columns tallied massive amounts of income, while others listed its few losses. One, in particular, caught Stella's attention:

Macarthur & Sons Waste Pickup & Disposal, Ltd.

Nov. 15, 1898. BLACK LIQUOR—18 tonnes.

Stella looked down and saw later entries of
the same nature logged every month thereafter.
She turned another page and blinked as some loose
papers fell out of the binding. They had been
wedged between sections—whether by accident or on
purpose, Stella could not say—but their subject was
plain enough.

Stella felt her head reel. She braced herself
on the desk, the truth dawning on her in one sudden rush. Once the library stopped spinning around
her, she looked to the nearest wall. It contained a
framed black-and-white photograph of the Bellows
brood—sans Sarah, naturally. They all stood posed
on the edge of the river that bisected the valley,
with their mill looming on the banks behind them. To
Stella, the only thing that looked more unnatural
than the Bellows' sour faces was the water itself.
It may have been an optical illusion caused by the
high-contrast snapshot, but the river's currents
appeared as still and black as tar.

The library door exploded inward, and an apo-
plectic Deodat tore inside, his face bloodred and
sweating. He pointed a fat finger at Stella and
shouted, "She's here! Going through our business!"

He lunged, but Stella dropped the journal and
avoided his swiping hands. She bolted past Deodat
and back into the hall, seeing the others' shadows streaking along the walls toward her. Stella
took off in the other direction, paying mind to the
defaced family portrait as she blew past it and
screamed, "Ramón! Where are you?"

She couldn't quite explain why she felt the overriding urge to be with him in that moment. Stella
and Ramón had only met on Halloween. Yet the bond
they'd shared—and the terrors they'd encountered—
since then had drawn them closer together than any

other pair Stella had ever seen. Even her own parents. As she ran, it struck Stella how her thoughts,
in what were likely her final moments, didn't
involve her long-lost mom. Rather, they were of the
one person who ever seemed to truly get Stella. The
one person who chased after—and was chased by—
ghosts of his own...

Stella's flight led her to the stately dining
room, its crystal chandeliers twinkling, its fine
china set on the long table with artful precision.
Frantic, she looked for some sort of exit, a doorway
to the kitchen or a butler's entrance, but saw none.
And the sideboards and cutlery hutches were far
too small to hide her.

As if sensing her fear, a young girl walked out
from the corner in which she'd been patiently waiting.
Dressed in a miniature version of a maid's uniform,
the girl stopped in front of the dining table and gestured under the linen cloth. Stella recognized those
blind eyes and the kind soul behind them.

Lou Lou, thought Stella.

They'd met once before in Stella's own time, when
Lou Lou was no longer a young servant but a senile
old woman. And the way little Lou Lou now smiled at
Stella, it nearly seemed as if she shared the same
recollection.

But that can't be, Stella reasoned. *That shouldn't
be possible. None of this should be possible.*

Stella nodded in gratitude and scrambled under
the table. Lou Lou nodded back imperceptibly, then
smoothed out the immaculate linen a second before
the Bellows descended upon the dining room.

"Did you hear her?" Delanie asked.

"No, ma'am," Stella heard young Lou Lou say on
the other side of the tablecloth.

"She's a liar," said Deodat.

"You wouldn't lie to us, Lou Lou," added Delanie.

Stella froze in place under the table. She'd been running from Deodat, his sons, and the violence of which she knew they were capable. Yet something in Delanie's voice stirred an even deeper fear within Stella. For the better part of ten years, she'd believed the worst a mother could do was abandon her child. Now, though, Stella wasn't so sure...

"No, ma'am," Lou Lou lied again.

Huddling under the table, Stella clenched her jaw to stop her chattering teeth—and to stave off the odd impulse to laugh. In all of her running and hiding, she hadn't yet made the connection. She was living her own scary story, much as Auggie and Chuck and the others had before her.

Sarah's book vanished from Stella's hands the instant Stella found herself transported to Sarah's time. It was as if the book, which had already consumed so many of Stella's feverish thoughts, had now finished the job by swallowing the rest of Stella into its pages. She wondered if Sarah's book still lay open on the floor of the Bellows' ruined foyer in good old 1968. If someone else—maybe Ramón, please let it be Ramón—had beat their own long odds of survival and found it there. If they were now reading the last chapter in Stella's life, which had now become entwined with Sarah's last chapter.

The writer in Stella had to admire the irony, the symmetry. After a lifetime spent chasing the ghost that had vacated her own home, Stella had now sublimated into a ghost herself. It wasn't Sarah Bellows who was haunting Stella any more. It was the other way around. Stella was the spirit that turned the Bellows estate into a haunted house.

The tablecloth ripped away beside Stella, and the younger Bellows brother, this one as thin and austere as his mother, roared, "You can't hide from us!"

Stella screamed as he dragged her out from

under the table. She kicked and thrashed, trying to free herself, but the protestations only succeeded in knocking off Stella's glasses. One of the others—Stella couldn't tell which with her blurred vision—then stepped on the lenses, cracking them as the rest of the Bellows took hold of her. They each grabbed one of Stella's limbs and hoisted her out of the dining room.

"She knows about the water," the eldest Bellows boy said, his tone devoid of sympathy.

"Then she'll know about the kids," said Delanie, her affect equally flat.

The younger brother clamped his free hand over Stella's face and said, "You're gonna shut your ugly mouth, or we're gonna shut it for ya!"

Stella tried to keep her wits, tried to keep track of her location within the mansion. Even without her glasses, she could tell where they were taking her. Entering the plating kitchen, Deodat took over restraining Stella while Delanie crossed over to one of the walls. Her bony fingers found purchase on a groove in the wood planks and exposed the inlaid lock. In spite of her mounting dread, Stella marveled at the deadbolt. It looked new and unworn, so different from the corroded hardware she and Ramón had discovered on Halloween night. Delanie pushed open the hidden door, and the men in her life hauled Stella toward it.

"Back where you belong," said the older brother.

"I'm not Sarah! I'm not Sarah!" Stella cried.

"Be quiet, or you know what you get," Delanie said dispassionately.

"I'm not her..." Stella went on, weaker this time. "Please ... you have to believe me ..."

If any of the Bellows heard her, they didn't show it. Deodat and his sons crossed through the doorway, taking Stella with them into the bowels of their

home. Railing against her captors, Stella slowed
their herky-jerky path down the cellar stairs somewhat, but still they managed to reach the catacombs.

"I'm not her," Stella moaned. "I'm not..."

The Bellows continued their impassive march
toward Sarah's subterranean bedroom. Delanie swung
open the reinforced door, and the others tossed
Stella into the chamber. Tears welled in her eyes,
making Stella's sight all the poorer, and she hollered, "I'm not Sarah! I'm not Sarah!"

"I warned you," Delanie said to the girl she mis-
took for her daughter. "Put up a fight, you don't
deserve the light."

With that, Mrs. Bellows shut off the basement's
already dismal lights, plunging Stella and her cell
into abject darkness. Stella wailed, but the only
response she heard was Delanie locking the bedroom
door from the outside.

"Please ... please..." Stella pleaded.

She modulated her gasps, careful not to hyper-
ventilate in these closed confines. And in doing so,
Stella heard another noise.

Breathing.

Faint. Labored. And not her own.

Stella's strained eyes finally adjusted, detecting
motion at the far end of the barred cage that doubled as a bedroom stripped of all comforts. Shadows
moved against shadows, gliding together and taking
shape. Backing into a corner, Stella watched in dis-
belief as the blackness coalesced into the body of
Sarah Bellows.

"Tell us a story, Sarah," said a child.

Stella jumped in place. The voice, innocent and
eager, came from right behind her, in the direction of the basement windows that offered a par-
tial view to the estate's moonlit grounds. She tilted
her head and heard more kids call out to the entity

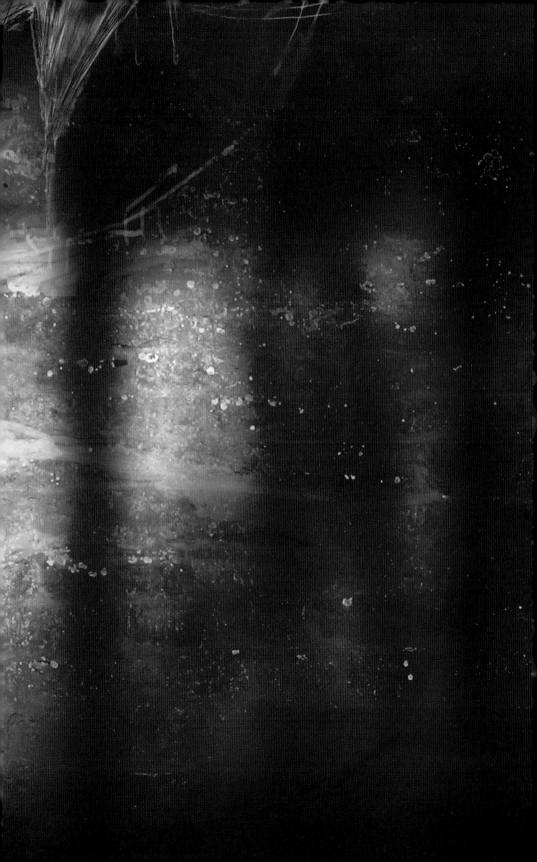

manifesting in the cellar.

"Tell us a scary one," begged another unseen child.

"Tell us," said a third.

Sarah Bellows's chalky form glowed almost phosphorescently in the gloom. She stood erect, and Stella could see that Sarah had been sitting in one of the room's few pieces of furniture, a rocking chair. The spirit glided toward Stella, who recoiled in terror, accidentally backing into a rickety, ramshackle bookcase. Its shelves collapsed, spilling several dog-eared tomes onto Stella. But one in particular landed right on her lap. It was Sarah Bellows notebook, its binding and cover in pristine condition and about seventy years younger than the one Stella had been carrying since Halloween. As Sarah drifted inexorably closer, Stella picked up the notebook and opened it to a blank page. In doing so, she felt an urgent and direct connection to—

"Ramón," Stella whispered.

For the second time that night, she wondered if he held the same book in their own time. Stella wrenched shut her eyes, which felt so vulnerable without their glasses, and thought she could perceive Ramón's voice, just as she heard those disembodied children's. Through the distance and the decades, she heard him and his insistent urgings that Stella tell a new story—to Sarah.

Whether a hallucination or not, the message galvanized Stella. She pulled Ramón's Zippo lighter from her jacket pocket and ignited it. Flickering light illuminated the enclosed space and the chilling, bone-white ghost that stared back at her. Stella shuddered, steadied herself, and said, "Sarah Bellows wasn't the monster everyone made her out to be..."

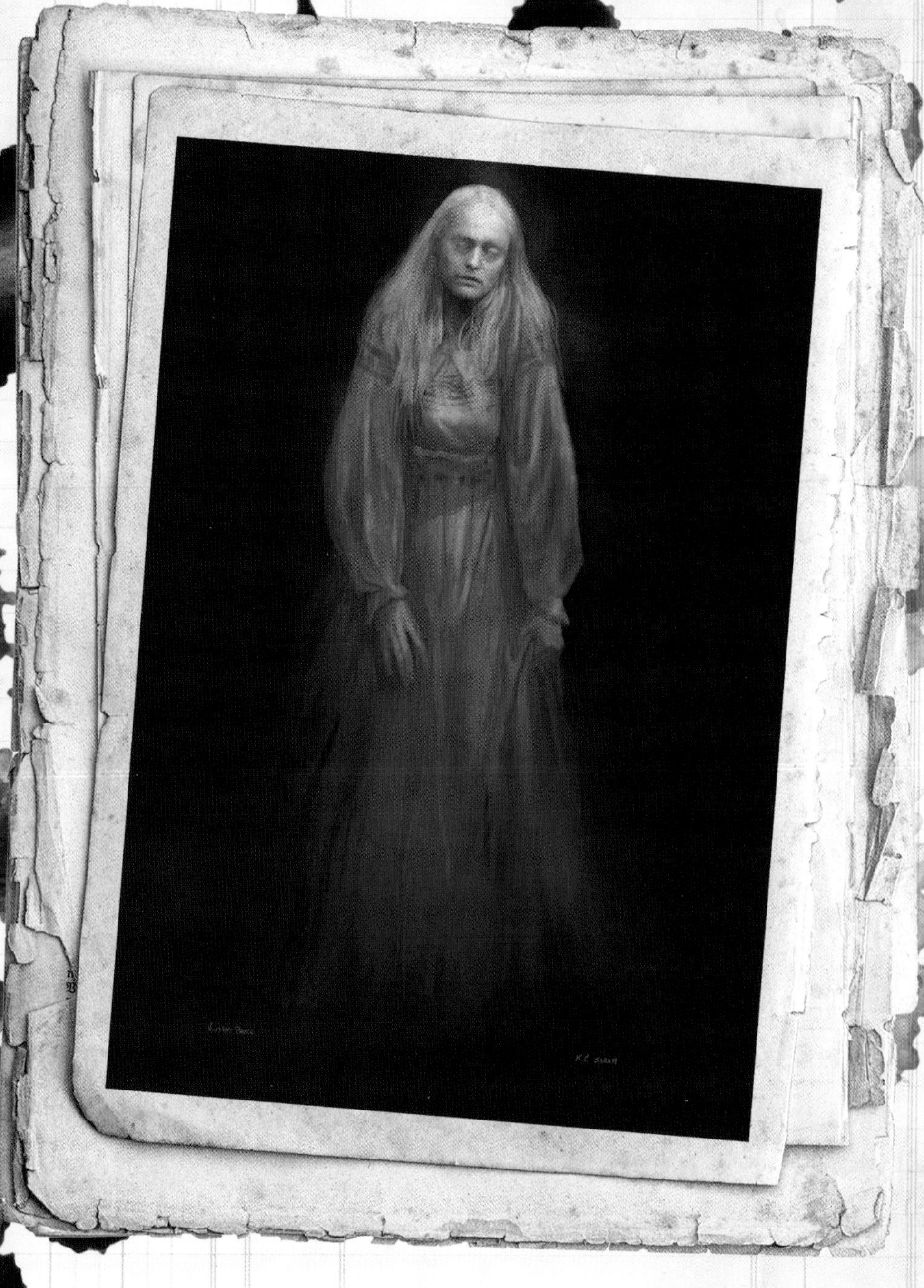

The Zippo extinguished, and Stella depressed its starter several times in quick succession before the tiny flame lit again. Sarah Bellows's spirit floated closer still. Willing herself not to scream again, Stella remembered what she'd pieced together in the family's library, and resumed her story.

"When children started disappearing, it was easy to blame the girl who never left the house..." said Stella, noting the iron shackles Sarah's family had screwed into the cellar walls. "But it wasn't Sarah who killed the children. It was her family."

The ghost of Sarah Bellows opened wide her mouth and unleashed a banshee's howl. The force of the shriek blew out the lighter and sent Stella scrambling behind one of the poles that supported the estate overhead. She fumbled with the Zippo some more, catching brief, strobing glimpses of Sarah's specter drawing nearer with each strike of the flint.

"The paper mill poisoned the river," Stella said, talking over the clicking lighter. "When the kids got sick, your family hid the truth. To protect themselves, they allowed everyone to believe *you* killed those children—the same children who had once visited you, who had called down through these basement windows to hear more of your stories."

A new flame finally sputtered to life, and Stella's heart skipped a beat. Sarah hovered before her, mere inches from Stella's face. The phantom's pallor resolved slightly, and Stella's eyes strained to make out the blur's features. With Sarah's long, ivory hair floating in the air between them, a pair of curious eyes stood revealed, their gaze far away with the flood of painful memories. Stella averted her own eyes and added, "All the stories everyone told about you. All the things they said. All the things I said."

The Zippo went out, the last of its fuel spent, and the shadows reclaimed the cellar. But Stella didn't even bother trying to restart the lighter. She accepted it, just as she accepted the fellow ghost who haunted this house alongside her. Sarah's lingering presence brought an unexpected sense of reassurance to Stella. She hadn't remembered feeling this secure since she was a little girl, nestled under the blankets while her mother recited another bedtime tale. So, Stella went on. Stella told her scary story in the dark.

"Our lies made you believe you were the monster," she said to Sarah. "But it isn't true. We are the monsters. We told the stories. We are the ones who did this to you."

In her mind's eye, Stella saw her younger self peek out from under those blankets, only to find that her mother was now gone. But for the first time in ten years, Stella felt the guilt—the blame she'd placed on herself at age six and that compelled her to chase the ghost of her abbreviated childhood ever since—suddenly go slack. For better or for worse, Stella Nicholls's and Sarah Bellows's conjoined stories somehow began and ended here at the foundations of Mill Valley's original sin.

"I'm sorry..." Stella sobbed. "I'm so sorry..."

She expected these to be her last words. But rather than inflict some gruesome demise, Sarah's translucent figure offered Stella something else instead—a silver fountain pen. With a subtle, ethereal gesture, Sarah indicated that Stella should take it and write with it.

Stella regarded the pen for a long moment, watching how it glinted in the shadows almost as brightly as the spirit that held it. But this hesitation was only temporary. Taking the pen from Sarah's hand, Stella pressed its point to the tip of her finger and bit her lip. Several red beads dribbled forth from under the skin, glistening

darkly in the lightless cellar. Stella dipped the
pen into her blood and began writing in the notebook of Sarah Bellows.

You are not the monster, Sarah. You never were.

The written words seemed to absolve both subject
and author of their respective losses. Sarah reached
out, not in malice, but to brush aside a wisp of
hair on Stella's bowed head. The gentleness of the
touch made Stella look up, and what she saw now was
not some remorseless revenant, but the real Sarah—a
lovely and loving albino girl wearing the trium-
phant expression of one who has finally been not
just heard but also understood.

"You weren't to blame," Stella told her. "It wasn't
your fault. It wasn't your fault..."

Although Stella couldn't be sure if that was meant
for someone else ... or for herself. She thought one
last time of her mother, of the void Dinah Nicholls
left in her absence, and broke down crying.

Sarah lifted her counterpart's tear-streaked
face in her lambent hand and smiled sweetly before
withdrawing into the shadows. Stella blinked, and in
that split second, her surroundings reverted once
again to their modern conditions. The cellar door,
locked in 1898, hung open and rotted, just as she'd
left it on Halloween. Stella started toward it, then
noticed something both new and old sprawled in the
middle of her path.

A skeleton rested peacefully on the basement
floor, powdery garments clinging to its ribs, tan-
gled white hair fanning from its skull. She knelt
beside these remains and placed the book she'd been
holding under the two folded, bony hands, returning the scary stories to their rightful owner.

Stella then dusted her hands of the past and
walked out of the cellar, ready to write her own
next chapter.

167

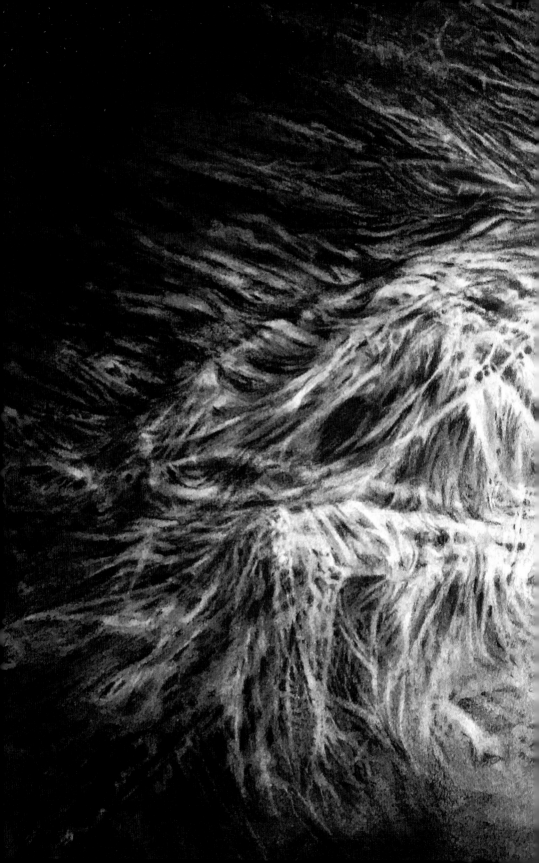

All scary stories start somewhere. This one begins in a bookstore in San Antonio, Texas.

That's where future filmmaker Guillermo del Toro first discovered *Scary Stories to Tell in the Dark*, not long after its first publication in 1981. Written by Alvin Schwartz, *Scary Stories* paired classic folklore and urban legends with macabre illustrations by artist Stephen Gammell, and aimed them at an audience of young readers hungry for their first taste of true horror fiction.

Schwartz's chilling stories and Gammell's vivid drawings fascinated and terrified children—as well as a teenage Del Toro, who says he instantly became a fan. "It retold the stories so beautifully, and Gammell's art was suitably spooky," del Toro explains. "It had a flavor all of its own. So, I became quite taken with it more than thirty years ago."

Thirty years later, del Toro has cowritten and produced a film adaptation of *Scary Stories to Tell in the Dark*, one that honors Schwartz's anthology structure and Gammell's nightmarish imagery in a clever way. It takes the idea of a book of scary stories with an otherworldly power to prey on the

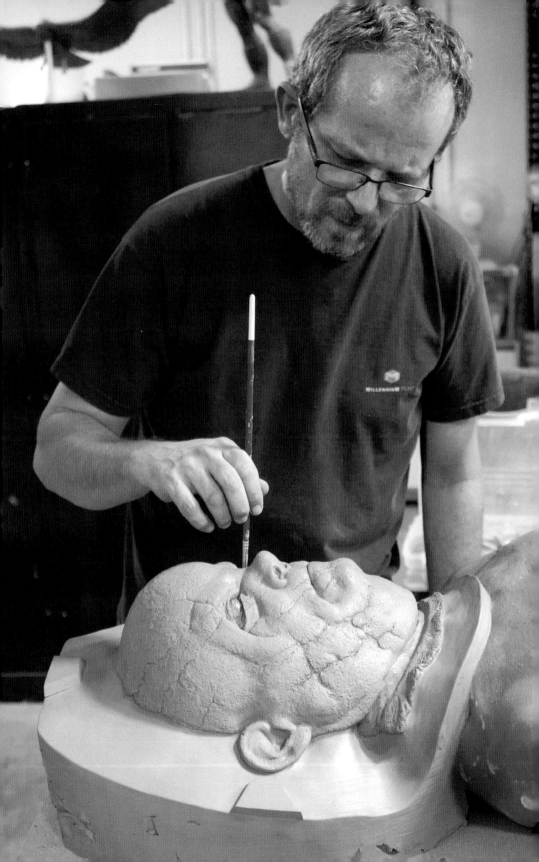

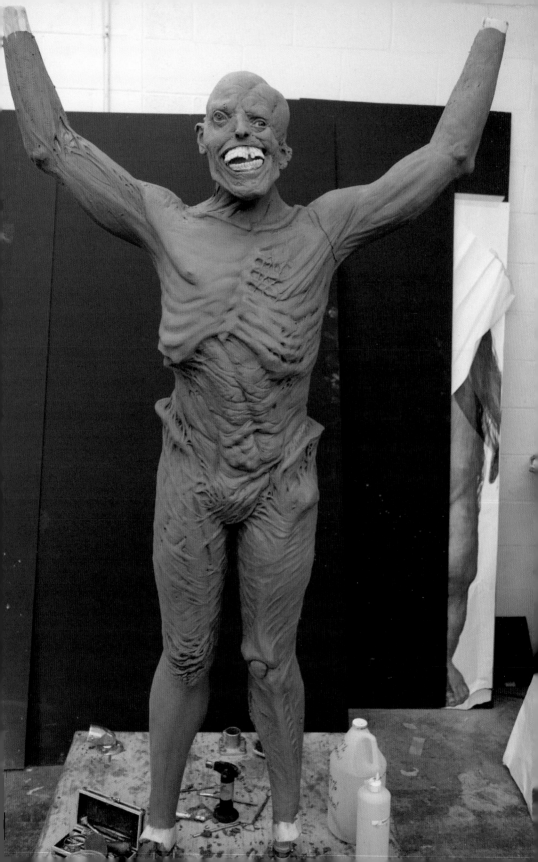

fears of kids and makes it literal—in the form of a supernatural journal that once belonged to a girl named Sarah Bellows.

As del Toro explains, "This book has short, scary stories in which Sarah basically trapped everybody that did her wrong. She was maligned by everybody in town as a witch, as somebody that had killed kids. She leaves this book behind that reads you—making you live a story specifically for you, something you fear, something you have avoided and need to confront."

Sarah's book is found in 1968 by a group of Pennsylvania teenagers who then must try to survive their encounters with its living stories—each of which is directly inspired by some of the most memorable creatures in Schwartz and Gammell's books, including del Toro's personal pick for the scariest of the scary stories: "Harold," about a living scarecrow that chases its victim through a cornfield.

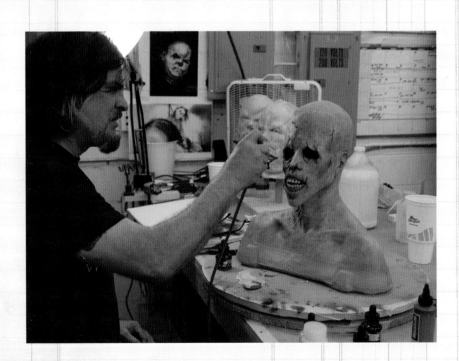

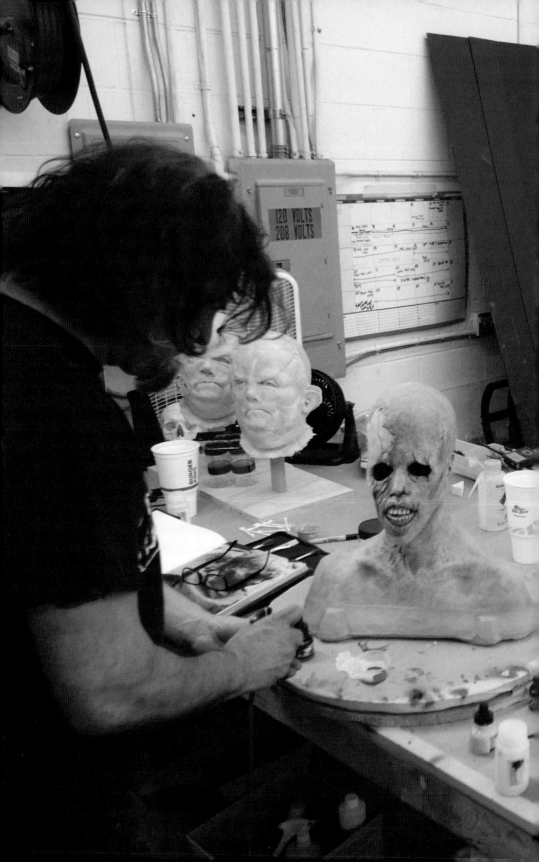

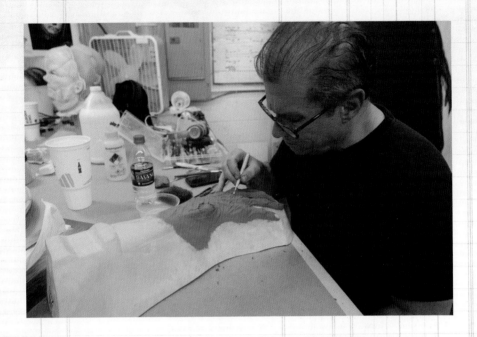

To help him bring these iconic horror tales to
life, del Toro recruited Norwegian filmmaker André
Øvredal to direct the *Scary Stories* movie. Del Toro
loved Øvredal's debut feature, *Trollhunter*, and
reveals he was his first choice for the job. "The
cinematic storytelling is very stylish in his movies,
but he doesn't overstylize," del Toro notes.

What followed was a unique collaboration
between two distinct horror sensibilities. Sometimes
the results onscreen are literally a combination of
their two aesthetics. Costume designer Ruth Myers
says Øvredal initially wanted the ghost of Sarah
Bellows dressed in a kind of Victorian straitjacket,
while del Toro preferred a more baroque dress. "I
felt that if I really put my mind to it," Myers says,
I could please everybody. So it's now a baroque
Victorian straitjacket dress."

In creating an overall look for *Scary Stories*,
Øvredal says, he became "obsessed" with incorpo-
rating Gammell's compositions into the film. "The
stories are great fun," Øvredal notes. "But the drawings are obviously a lot of what's scary about these
books. I was thinking initially that they would be
digital creatures. But Guillermo convinced me very
early on that we have to do this for real."

That meant bringing in the artists at Spectral
Motion, which del Toro calls "one of the last great
remaining effects houses in the world." Using a creative process del Toro developed on *Hellboy II*,
sculptors were assigned to work on specific creatures from the beginning of preproduction all the
way to the end of shooting. "You don't have a guy
sculpting, a guy molding, a guy painting, a guy
dressing," del Toro explains. "The same person that
sculpted it is the person that paints it, that dresses
it, and is the person on set."

That precisely controlled process yielded sin-
gularly fearsome monsters like sculptor Norman
Cabrera's digit-impaired corpse from Schwartz and
Gammell's "The Big Toe." For the eerie, lurching
Harold, del Toro says, he instructed Cabrera to
drain his design of colors in order to mimic the
effect of years of sun on a real scarecrow, until
he's "kind of bleached and dirty and has bugs living
inside him."

The degree to which the *Scary Stories* team was
able to transform Gammell's inky, surreal artwork
into three-dimensional creatures is truly remark-
able. They turned "The Red Spot," about a young
woman's encounter with a rapidly-expanding spider
bite, into a prosthetic makeup effect so harrowing
it could give a dermatologist a panic attack. Mike
Hill, who sculpted the creature from del Toro's
Oscar-winning film *The Shape of Water*, designed
the ghastly jigsaw puzzle of human limbs that the

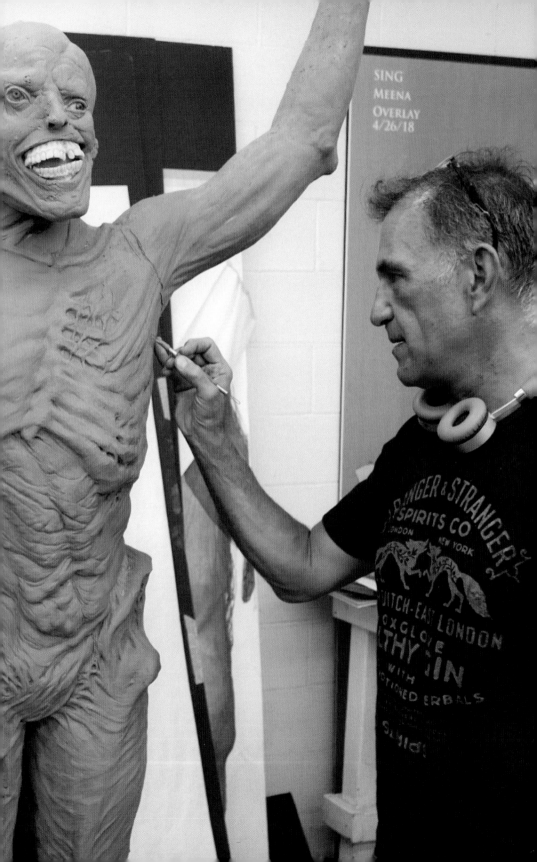

SING
MEENA
Overlay
4/26/18

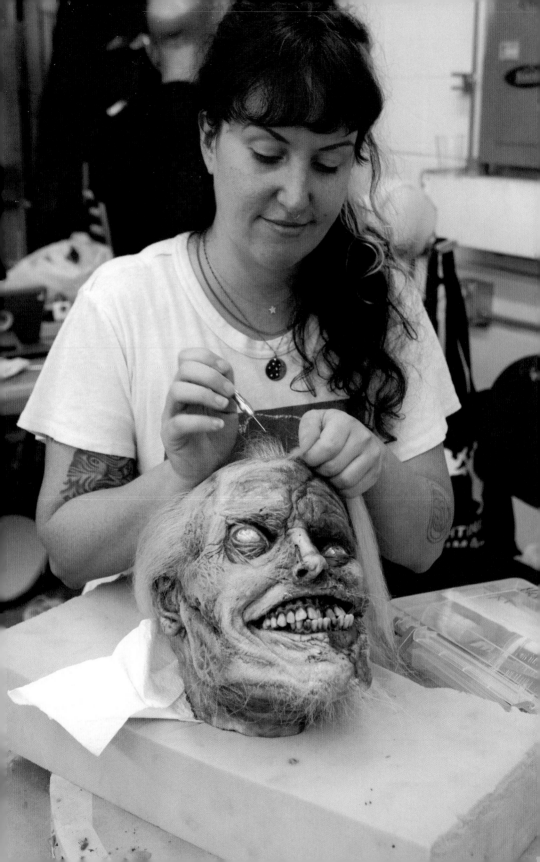

filmmakers dubbed "the Jangly Man," as well as "the Pale Lady"—a disturbingly genial phantom that looks like it just stepped out Gammell's drawing for the short story "The Dream."

In the world of the film, all of these specters spring from the journal of Sarah Bellows, which is hidden in the catacombs beneath the dilapidated Bellows house, which becomes one of the movie's signature locations. Hoping to avoid the cliché of a "typical horror-movie Victorian house," production designer David Brisbin found a real old home in Ontario that he says "reeks of wealthy industrial evil baron" and then paired it with meticulously detailed interiors built on a soundstage. Brisbin's sets not only lent scenes a spooky atmosphere, they were also accurate to the period in which the Bellows house would have been built. (Look closely, Brisbin confesses, and you'll see the walls are covered with a devil-themed wallpaper that was actually sold in the 1880s.)

In the end, Øvredal says, he wants audiences to leave the Bellows house and his *Scary Stories* with "sweaty palms," feeling like "they've been scared for two hours by an epic, timeless" horror film. Del Toro hopes viewers will take those feelings even further. "Scary narratives," he explains "are essential to a young adult. They tell a kid there is adversity, and there are these antidotes to adversity. Feeling fear is natural. Vanquishing it is extraordinary." Perhaps someday we'll be reading about an artist who was driven to create something extraordinary by their feelings for the new *Scary Stories*, just as del Toro was by his feelings for the original three decades ago.

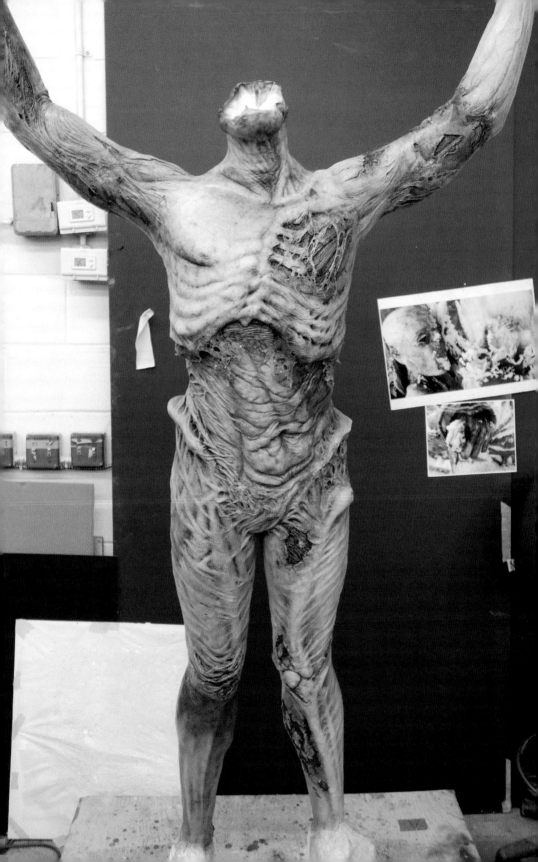

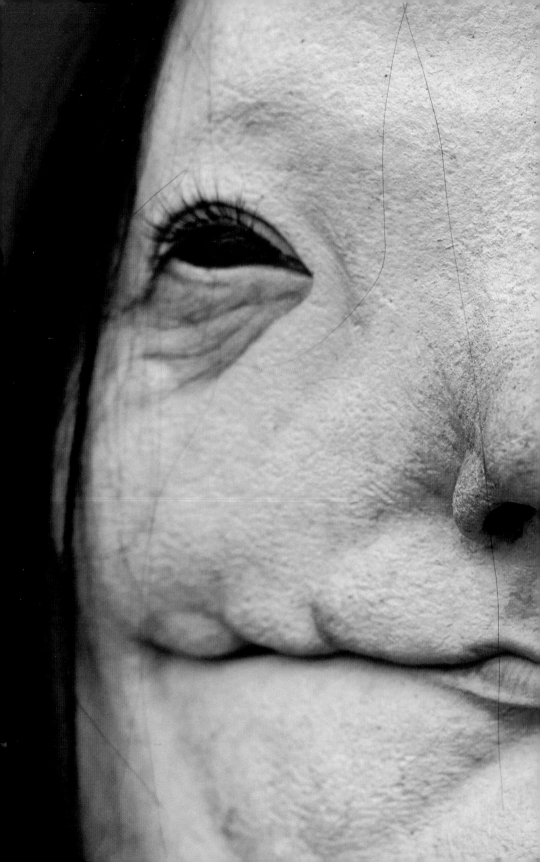

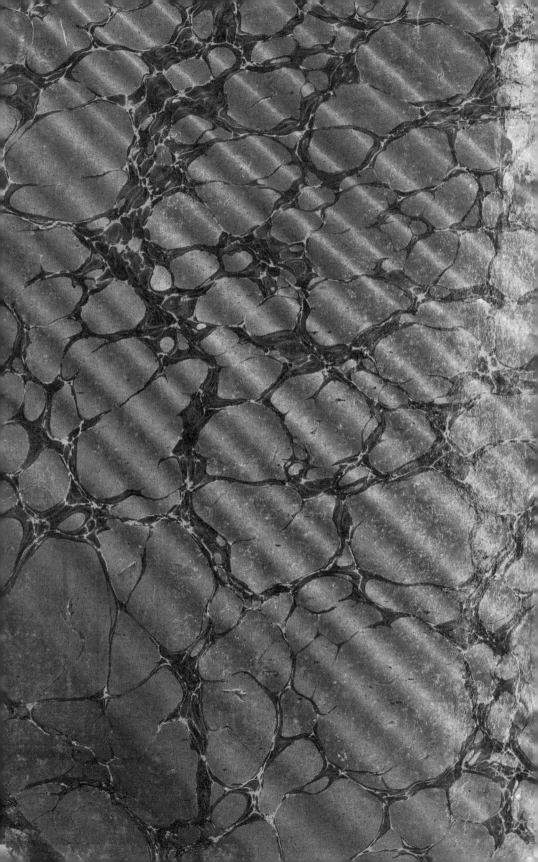